THE CAVALIER KING
CHARLES SPANIEL

POPULAR DOGS' BREED SERIES

*

THE CAVALIER KING CHARLES SPANIEL

MARY FORWOOD

POPULAR DOGS
London Melbourne Sydney Auckland Johannesburg

Popular Dogs Publishing Co. Ltd

An imprint of the Hutchinson Publishing Group

17–21 Conway Street, London W1P 6JD

Hutchinson Group (Australia) Pty Ltd
16–22 Church Street, Hawthorn, Melbourne, Victoria 3122, Australia

Hutchinson Group (NZ) Ltd
32–34 View Road, PO Box 40-086, Glenfield, Auckland 10

Hutchinson Group (SA) Pty Ltd
PO Box 337, Bergvlei 2012, South Africa

First published 1967
Second edition, revised 1972
Third edition, revised 1974
Fourth edition, revised 1978
Fifth edition, revised 1980
Sixth edition, revised 1983
Seventh edition, revised 1985

Set in Baskerville by Book Ens, Saffron Walden, Essex

© Mary Forwood 1967, 1972, 1974, 1978, 1980, 1983, 1985

Printed and bound in Great Britain by Anchor Brendon Ltd,
Tiptree, Essex

British Library Cataloguing in Publication Data
Forwood, Lady Mary
    The Cavalier King Charles spaniel.—7th ed.
    —(popular dogs' breed series)
    1. Cavalier King Charles spaniels
    I. Title   II. Series
    636.7'52   SF429.C36

ISBN 0 09 151551 3

ACKNOWLEDGEMENTS

Throughout the writing of this book I have received nothing but help and kindness from those to whom I have applied, and I would like publicly to acknowledge their help and give them my sincere gratitude.

To the Kennel Club and all its staff, for not only giving me access to anything I wanted but for putting up with many telephone calls to look up something that I had forgotten.

To Mr Peter Barnes for so kindly doing the anatomical drawings.

To my veterinary surgeon who so kindly checked what I had written in Chapter 8.

To the late Constance, Duchess of Westminster, the late Earl of Pembroke, Lord Methuen and the Wallace Collection for so kindly letting me reproduce pictures from their collections. To all those breeders both in this country and abroad who have so generously lent me pictures of their dogs, and to Mrs Burrows of Thomas Fall, and C. M. Cooke who have taken some of these photographs.

To Mme C. Van den Boom (Holland); Mrs Jay Albrecht (America); Mrs Matherson (New Zealand); Miss Reading and Mrs Hendry (Australia); Frau Östergren (Sweden); Mrs Nugent (Ireland); Mr T. Lawson (South Africa), and Mrs Konkle (Canada), all of whom have taken immense trouble over getting Cavalier news for me from their respective countries. To Miss Valda Salmon, whose fascinating list of pictures portraying Cavaliers has been such a help to me and whose notes on the history of the breed have also been so helpful. To Mrs D. Maclean who has done so much typing for me.

And finally to my husband, who has on many occasions had to put up with a thoroughly bad-tempered wife when she frequently realized that writing was not really her *métier* in life.

M.F.

CONTENTS

ILLUSTRATIONS

ILLUSTRATIONS

IN THE TEXT

AUTHOR'S INTRODUCTION

It was a great honour to be asked to write this book on Cavaliers, and I only hope it is not a matter of misplaced faith.

Cavaliers are such a popular breed now that it is rewarding to trace their tremendous increase since the breed first started its Club in 1928.

I have sifted through the large amount that was written, particularly about King Charles and his spaniels, so that a moderately clear picture will emerge of their history. It is sometimes impossible to state a fact categorically and one can only quote the writers of bygone days in the hope that they were accurate.

I have tried to be practical in the chapters on puppy rearing, weaning and general management, and I hope that what I have written will be of some help to pet owners and novices, and that perhaps even the more experienced breeders may be able to pick out something that will be of use to them.

Admittedly it must be of great interest to Cavalier breeders today to see how the old champions and the present-day winners resemble each other. I feel very strongly that, as the breed has increased enormously and a lot of novices have come into our midst (sadly quite a few of the old established breeders have passed away), it would be wise for the new generation not to try to run before it can walk.

Some bad faults have manifested themselves in the last few years, one of which is very faulty hind movement. A spaniel is a working dog and without being structurally well conformed it cannot work as it was built to do. Straight stifles must prevent a working dog moving as it should do, and I can only hope that present-day breeders will be aware of this fact and breed for this natural result – it is so easy to ruin a breed and so difficult to improve it. However, I am sure that the many breeders with the good of the Cavalier in their hearts will carry on the tremendous work to which those early breeders dedicated themselves and that the breed will reach an even higher standard than it has today. Do not forget it is one of the top Toy breeds, so it is up to all of us to keep the flag flying.

For this sixth edition I have again revised the chapter on Cavaliers Abroad and brought all three appendices up to date. The photograph of the 1973 Cruft's Supreme Best in Show winner first appeared in the third edition (1974), two or three more new photographs were included in the fourth (1978) edition and there are three new ones in this edition.

Burley, Hants.   M.F.
1983

1
Cavaliers through the Centuries

THERE has always been and always will be speculation as to the correct ancestry of the Cavalier. We do know that the Toy Spaniel is an ancient breed and certainly was in England in the Tudor days. Queen Mary is reputed to have had one of the Blenheim variety in 1554. These little spaniels were undoubtedly the Toy Spaniels which were well known on the Continent in the fifteenth, sixteenth and seventeenth centuries. They were small, with a flat top to their head, a pointed nose, a long feathery coat, and look as though they weighed around ten to twelve pounds. They may have originated in Spain, Italy, Holland or France. There is Titian's (c. 1477–1576) painting of the Duchess of Urbino which is probably the earliest glimpse that we have of the Toy Spaniel and inclines us to believe that perhaps the romantic seaport of Venice was the birthplace of these fascinating little dogs.

Conversely, before Cavaliers, or rather Toy Spaniels, appeared on canvas they were to be seen in tapestries. In the Louvre there is a very fine fifteenth-century Arras tapestry called *The Offering of the Heart*. In the foreground of this tapestry is what is obviously a Toy Spaniel exactly like our present-day Cavaliers. The colours are faded and it is impossible to tell if it was a Blenheim, Tricolour or Black/White, but it does prove that they were in existence in the fifteenth century.

The first picture that appears in England was that of Queen Mary I and her husband Philip of Spain with a pair of spaniels lying at their feet. It was painted by Antonio Moro in 1554 and is now the property of the Duke of Bedford and hangs in Woburn Abbey.

There is an entry in the Privy Purse expenses of the Queen which is as follows: 'Gevene to Sir Brian Tuke, servante, bringing a couple of little fayre hounds to my lade's grace 5/–.'

What exactly that entry means is anyone's guess. It would appear that the Toy Spaniels of that day were mainly Brown and White and Black and White. In 1563, when Mary Queen of Scots was beheaded, a small Black/White dog was found under her skirts. This is generally thought to have been a Cavalier. In the narrative of the execution endorsed in Lord Burghley's hand and forwarded from Fotheringay to the Court, it is recorded: 'Then one of the executioners, pulling off her garters, espied her little dogg which was crept under her clothes which could not be gotten forth but by force, yet afterwards would not departe from the dead corpse, but came and lay between her head and her shoulders, which being inbued with her bloode, was caryed away and washed, as all things ells were that had any bloode was either burned or clean washed'. Probably she brought either this little dog or its ancestor with her when she returned to Scotland from France.

Baroness Wentworth in her well-known book *Toy Dogs and their Ancestors* has definitely traced a Dutch variety of spaniel more than a hundred years before Charles II had them, and they were probably brought to this country by Anne of Cleves and later by William of Orange.

Another source says it was almost certain the spaniel came from Spain and one theory is that they were bred from a class of cocker or sporting spaniel, reduced in size by 'in-and-in' breeding.

The little dogs were bred in considerable numbers before Charles II; indeed, there is a reference to them by Dr Caius, Physician to Queen Elizabeth I, by various names, 'Comforter', 'Fisting Curre' or 'Fisting Hound'. It is thought that the so-called spaniels which were fostered and petted by the aristocracy were a more mongrel type of dog with spaniel characteristics with not a great deal of colouring, but what there was was either red or liver. These little dogs were often carried by the nobility for warmth. On the long carriage journeys they were placed on the stomach and it was considered that they relieved pain and discomfort; hence the use of the name 'Comforter'.

There was obviously more than one type of Toy Spaniel in

those days. Buffon in 1750 says that England had black spaniels called Gredius and he gave the name of 'Pyrame' to such Gredius that had 'fire-marks', i.e. tan markings over the eyes, on muzzle, throat and legs. This sounds very similar to the Black/Tans of today.

There was also a small all-black curly Toy Spaniel which was bred either from the Spanish Truffle dog or else from a variety of small water spaniels. It would seem more than likely that these curly dogs were mated with the other Toy Spaniels and produced the Black/Tan. This would account for the curly coat that a lot of the Black/Tans used to have. When King Charles I was walking across the Park to the place of execution in Whitehall he was accompanied by a little spaniel called Rogue. One of the Roundheads kidnapped this little spaniel and placed it on public exhibition for profit that same evening, but nothing is known as to what eventually happened to that poor little dog.

As far as is known by all the paintings there were only the three colours in Charles II's time – the Brown/White, Black/White and Tricolour.

The small black spaniel which is pictured in Van Dyck's painting *The Family of Charles I* was probably a Gredin.

The first authentic information concerning a Tricolour comes from the *London Gazette* of October 1667. It reads: 'Lost in Dean's Yard, Westminster, on 25 October, a young white spaniel about 6 months old, with a black head, red eyebrows and a black spot on his back. Belonging to His Highness Prince Rupert. If anyone can bring him to Prince Rupert's Lodgings in the Stone Gallerie at Whitehall, he shall be well rewarded for his pains.' This was just after Charles II had married Catherine of Braganza and been crowned king. She herself may have brought some spaniels over either from Portugal or Tangier which was part of her dowry.

Earlier than this the Japanese Spaniel had been introduced into England. In 1613 Captain Saris returned from Japan with dogs for the King as a present from the Emperor. These were most likely the Japanese Spaniel, and Catherine could also have brought some over because both the Dutch and Portuguese had contact with Japan.

Yet another theory is that the Toy Spaniel was a descendant of the Tibetan strain of 'Palace' dog and originated from China. There is a tale that somewhere around A.D. 900 the Emperor of China sent a present of two of his Royal and Holy Pekingese, known as the 'Palace' dogs, to the Dalai Lama of Lhasa, and from these two little dogs a strain from which the Toy Spaniel could have come was bred. They were then taken to the Spanish Peninsula by the first Portuguese explorer who reached China.

Van Dyck, Watteau, Boucher and Greuze all pictured a small animal – long-nosed, flat top to the head, curly tail and very active.

At the French Court many royal pictures were painted in which Toy Spaniels appeared. Charles II's sister, Henrietta of Orléans, who was brought up from a baby in France, is pictured by Pierre Miguard with one of these little dogs in her lap, this one is a red and white spaniel. There is also a picture of the Dauphin with a black dog and a Black/White one, and one of Louis XIV with a beautiful Black/White Toy Spaniel. The Black/White are also very prominent in Watteau's *Embarquement pour Cythere* and *La Toilette*, to mention only two of his pictures.

Wherever one goes one sees portraits by the Old Masters of families with their little dogs. Sir Peter Lely certainly painted two, one being a portrait of Dorothy, Lady Temple 'with her favourite spaniel' in 1678. It appears that she was a great devotee of the breed and owned many of them. The other portrait is of a Miss Skipwith, where the Toy Spaniel is almost life-sized.

Henri III of France also owned Toy Spaniels. We are told that he 'came across them in Italy after his flight from Poland', but whether this is true or not is conjecture, but he is certainly shown in at least one of his portraits with a spaniel. There was even a Toy Spaniel in the first illustrated edition of Shakespeare's works and it is to be found in an engraving of a scene depicting a quarrel from *The Taming of the Shrew*. The Toy Spaniel, or let us now call them 'Cavaliers', appears not in the least put out by crockery being smashed and upturned tables, but seems to be barking hard to encourage the quarrellers.

A whole chapter could be written on the portraits in which Cavaliers appeared, so they must have been universally popular and not just royal pets, although it is as royal dogs that we think most of them. To show that they were also the pets of the ordinary people I quote from the *Daily Courant* of 9 January 1720: 'Whereas a little black & white spaniel breed, about 6 months old (the white on his neck had been lately burned) broke loose out of Mr Nash's shop at Bishopsgate St. on Thursday last at 8 o'clock in the morning with a piece of red worsted garter about her neck, whoever has taken up the bitch and will bring her to the Sign of St Martin's in Yard Buildings shall have 5/– for their pains.'

The name Blenheim came from John, 1st Duke of Marlborough, and was given to the Liver and White Cavaliers so much favoured by him. To this day that particular colour has retained that name. He was supposed to have had a Cavalier with him at the battle of 'Blindheim' or 'Blenheim' (hence the name), which was fought on the north bank of the Danube near the little town of Hochstadt. His Blenheims appear to have been rather larger than the ordinary Cavalier and it is possible that he may have crossed them with some other spaniel to get them large enough for retrieving. They certainly appear larger in pictures. One theory is that he brought his Blenheims from Spain. Certainly according to legend he had them in England while he was fighting abroad. The legend of the spot is supposed to come from his Duchess, Sarah, who, sitting amongst her ladies at home, was in such a state of nervous tension awaiting news from the field at Blindheim that she pressed her thumb hard on the forehead of her spaniel bitch lying in her lap. Shortly afterwards the bitch whelped and the puppies were found to have a red lozenge the size of Her Grace's thumb on their foreheads. Although this is purely legendary, the spot or lozenge is a much valued thing in the breed today, and is a charming thought.

It has always been thought that King Charles Spaniels had certain privileges given to them during the time of Charles II. This is a delightful assumption and was no doubt true in the Carolean days by dint of their being royal dogs, but unfortunately nowhere in the Statute Book is any mention of any law allowing them access without argument to almost anywhere in the realm – or that they may travel free on any public transport. As there was hardly any public transport in those days this second law seems more unlikely than the first. Probably how the theory came about was because King Charles II was never without these dogs. Everywhere he went, much to the distress of many of his friends and courtiers, so went the dogs. He would have made it abundantly clear to anyone who dared say a word against them that it would be better if they kept their mouth shut and minded their own business.

Certainly Pepys in his *Diary* was no lover of them and on one occasion in September 1666, while describing a visit to the Council Chamber, writes:

'All I observed was the silliness of the King playing with his dogs all the while and not minding the business.' In 1867 Stonehenge reports that 'the old President of Magdalen College, who died about ten years ago in his hundredth year, was accustomed to say that when he was a little boy he had been told by an old lady that when she was a little girl she saw the King round the Magdalen walks with those little dogs'.

As hygiene was not a very strong point with the human race in that day and age, it seems hardly likely that anyone would have bothered much about putting dogs out or anything like that, so it is quite reasonable to suppose that those objectors to the spaniels probably had a certain amount of right on their side. The streets were in a filthy condition and one can imagine that dirty feet and an altogether muddy little dog on the chairs on which one had to sit dressed in the lovely materials of that age was not conducive to foster a great love. There is no doubt that Charles was ruled completely by his dogs and they were allowed to do exactly as they liked.

One more quotation from that period is from John Evelyn. He was a dog lover, but it seems that Charles's dogs were too much for him. When summing up the royal characteristics at the time of the Monarch's death, he wrote: 'He took delight in having a number of little spaniels follow him and lie in his bedchamber and where he often suffered the bitches to puppy and give suck which rendered it very offensive, and indeed made the whole Court nasty and stinking.' Charles's brother James II also adored Cavaliers, but on the fall of the Stuarts they went out of fashion. William and Mary, who were on the throne, were not the great Cavalier lovers that Charles and James were, and they preferred pugs.

Many of the Cavaliers followed their masters into exile and others remained at the country seats of some of the more powerful nobles. We know that Cavaliers were still in existence, although not in fashion, all through the early Georgian period. Zoffany paints two Cavaliers under a table in his picture of *The Garricks entertaining Dr Johnson*, so it would appear that not only did they move in the social set but also in literary circles.

In 1800 John Scott writes of the Duke of Marlborough's 'cocking spaniels'. These were obviously the larger type of Cavalier that he used for shooting. Stonehenge says that 'about the year 1841, perhaps two or three good specimens existed in the neighbourhood of Blenheim and only one of passing excellence – a bitch named Rose – her head exquisitely modelled and full of character and intelligence, was in exact proportion to her size, her coat was soft, silky, shiny and of transparent whiteness except where it was stained with a genuine rich Blenheim orange'. This orange colour varies with today's Standard, which calls for a rich chestnut colour, this latter having much more blue in it than the orange. This description of the Blenheim doesn't sound like a big dog at all, but it is so difficult to get a clear picture when there are so many contradictions.

In 1800 Sydenham Edwards writes: 'Marlboroughs are a small variety of cocker with blunt noses and very round heads and highly valued by sportsmen.'

This is a complete contradiction of every other description that we have had and is the first mention of anything to do with a round head. Certainly in Landseer's famous pictures of *A Lady with her Spaniels* and *The Cavaliers' Pets* there was no hint of a round head. He started the former in 1838, but didn't finish it until some years later and it was first exhibited in 1874. The latter picture was painted in two days and hung in the British Institution in 1845. The Cavaliers in this picture are certainly more substantial dogs than those in the very early pictures. Their faces have filled out to give that rather more gentle expression and they have more bone than their ancestors, but they are by no means large in any kind of way and are in perfect proportion.

Ruby-coloured Cavaliers, which are a rich red all over and should have no white on them, first appeared in 1850 and there is a portrait of the Duke and Duchess of Cumberland walking with their Ruby. They were always inclined to be coarser than the Blenheim or Tricolour, probably through the Black/Tan blood. The Black/Tans appear always to have been more domed-headed and a coarser type of spaniel. The first Ruby that appeared was owned by Mr Risum, but in 1875 a Mr Garwood (who was one of London's oldest fanciers) won a second prize with his Ruby dog Dandy at the Alexandra Palace Show. These must have been much more similar to the King Charles of today.

Some other breed of dog must have been introduced to produce the very short nose of the present-day King Charles. A bulldog has been suggested, but it seems more likely that a pug might have been used. Certainly not a pekingese, as they didn't come to England until after the Chinese War of 1860 and by that time the King Charles had become as it is now.

When a large specimen of the breed appears it is more than likely that this is a throw-back to the original Blenheims owned by the Duke of Marlborough. There can be no doubt that the Toy Spaniel included in so many of the old paintings must be an accurate picture, as all the painters have portrayed them in the same vein. They were also to be seen on the lids of those lovely gold and enamel boxes that the French of the eighteenth century made so beautifully, and in the china pieces that Rockingham and Stafford kilns produced, to mention only two of the famous china-makers.

There are several paintings portraying Queen Victoria as a young girl with her Tricolour Cavalier Dash. This appears to have been a small type of spaniel with high-set ears, long leathers and a pleasing expression. Dash seems to have been a much loved pet and there are even embroidered pictures which are supposed to represent him. As this little dog was so very obviously a Cavalier, it would seem that the cross took place later on in Queen Victoria's reign, but as far as is known there are no records of who instigated the cross. What Sydenham Edwards was writing about must have been another variety of spaniel.

It would be so much more satisfactory if more authentic information could be gathered regarding the true ancestry of our fascinating breed, but for the moment all we can do is to reconstruct to the best of our ability.

2

The Breed as it is Today

DURING the period of the late Victorian and Edwardian era Cavaliers such as we know them today were virtually extinct. There was a Toy Spaniel Club and the colours were then known by other names than today. The Black/Tans were King Charles, Rubies were just called Red, Prince Charles was the name given to Tricolours and the only one to remain as it is now was the Blenheim. They remained like this until 1923 when they all became King Charleses and the colours were named as they are today.

There were not many big breeders, the biggest and best known was Mrs Raymond Mallock who did a great deal for the King Charles breed.

It was really not until 1926 that any kind of move was made to breed back to the original type, and the incentive for this came from an American gentleman. Mr Roswell Eldridge visited this country in that year, and was horrified to find that the old type of Toy Spaniel which he had so admired had been replaced by the flat-nosed kind. He was determined that the Cavalier should come back in its rightful form and offered a prize of £25 for the Best Dog and £25 for the Best Bitch for five years running, for the best specimen exhibited in a class for Blenheim spaniels of the old type at Cruft's. The following is the quotation that appeared in the Cruft's Catalogue: 'As shown in the pictures of Charles II's time, i.e. a long face, no stop, flat skull not inclined to be "domed" and the spot in the centre of the skull.' Unfortunately Mr Eldridge died in America about the time when his prizes were coming to an end. In spite of this offer, and £25 meant a much larger sum of money than it does today, only two entries were made in the first year. However, a handful of exhibitors banded together with a view to forming a club with the object of reviving the old type of Toy Spaniel. These stalwarts included Mrs A. Pitt, Chairman for over thirty years with a gap of three years from 1963 to 1965 when Mr Harry White ably took over the reins, after which I was Chairman for six years. Now Mr Boardman is in the chair. Mrs Pitt was formerly a noted Chow Chow breeder but couldn't resist the challenge to revive a breed. With her in this venture were the well-known Pyrenean breeder Mme Harper Trois-Fontaines, and several others. When the Cavalier King Charles Spaniel Club was first registered in 1928 Mrs Pitt was its Secretary and the Chairman was Miss Mostyn Walker. In 1929 Mrs B. F. Thomas became the Club's Secretary and she remained in office until 1944 when Mrs J. Eldred took on the Secretaryship. A great deal of time was spent studying the old pictures and in drawing up the Standard of Points which every breed has to have under Kennel Club rules. This Standard was drawn up by very experienced breeders and the great idea was to make the Cavalier a natural little animal with no trimming, so that the professional dog world could not get at it and shape and trim it into something it was never meant to be. A certain amount of elasticity had to be allowed, as it was obvious that nowhere near a perfect specimen was going to be produced out of a new breed. There were, of course, few long-nosed dogs to be seen and the breeders had to use anything that the King Charles breeders threw out because it had too much nose. A popular thought is that a drop-eared Papillon was used to bring back the long nose and flat-topped head.

In those days sales were almost impossible and to sell the ones not wanted for breeding was a monumental task. If £2 was obtained the owner thought he had done very well indeed, so it can be seen that not only time but a great deal of money went into this little venture and the owners and breeders of today owe a great debt of gratitude to that small band of pioneers.

The name Cavalier King Charles was chosen, as obviously the name King Charles must remain somewhere in the title. These little dogs were shown in the same classes as the ordinary King Charles right up until 1945 when separate registrations and classifications were granted by the Kennel Club.

On Thursday 29 August 1946 came the great moment and culmination of all those years of hard work. The first Cavalier King Charles Spaniel Club Championship Show was held. The venue was the School of Drama, Alverston, Stratford-on-Avon, and the show manager was Mr A. O. Grindey, better known as the Secretary of the two Birmingham shows. Mr Cecil Oakley was the ring steward. At that time the Club's President was the Marchioness of Cambridge, whose close connection with the Royal Family made it a special compliment to the Club that she had consented to accept this office. The Chairman was Mrs Pitt and the Committee were Mrs B. Jennings, Mrs S. Massingham, Mrs D. Gordon, Mrs D. Murray, Mr V. Green, Mr H. Bawn and Mme J. Harper Trois-Fontaines. The Club's Secretary was Mrs J. Eldred. Altogether there were twenty-eight dogs entered and three litters, making a total of 109 entries plus nine in the Brace Class and three in the Team. The judge for this great event was Mrs Jennings, one of the original band of pioneers, and she made Mrs Eldred's Belinda of Saxham Best in Show. Belinda was a Blenheim bred by Mrs Eldred by Duke's Son out of Linooga. The Reserve Best Bitch went to Mrs Pitt's Comfort of Ttiweh. The Best Dog was Miss Jane Pitt's Daywell Roger by Cannonhill Richey out of Daywell Nell, destined to become the first and most famous champion in the breed so far. The Reserve Dog was Mrs Eldred's Jan of Turnworth.

There were five Club cups on offer, which was a great thrill. The following year there were two Club Championship Shows, the second one being held at Trinity Hall, Great Portland Street, London W1, where Mrs Mitchell was the judge, and there were fifty-two dogs entered; this was in May, but yet again in August at Hinchwick, the lovely home of Mr Roger Pilkington, another Championship Show was held. This time the judge was Mr Walter Worfolk and there were fifty-one dogs entered. Both these shows had more trophies presented and a great many specials, and it really looked as though Cavaliers were gaining a foothold. Mr A. O. Grindey was still the Show Secretary and the officers and Committee of the Club were still in office. The L.K.A. also had classes with certificates for Cavaliers that year, so that made three sets of C.C.s in 1947.

From then onwards as the registrations grew so were more sets awarded and more shows were putting on Cavalier classes. In the records at the Kennel Club sixty dogs were registered in 1946. This total was more than doubled to 134 in 1947 and the following year to 181. Since then the breed has gone up and up until now it is on the 3,500-a-year mark.

The first dog that really made its mark on the breed and had the correct long nose and flat top to its head was Ann's Son, bred by Miss Mostyn Walker. He was the sire of Daywell Nell, who herself was the dam of the famous Ch. Daywell Roger. Both these two animals were bred by Mrs Lawrence Brierley, who had the prefix Daywell. In all, Ch. Daywell Roger produced eleven champion sons and daughters and won seven C.C.s. Apart from those eleven sons and daughters he also had many grandchildren and great grandchildren who were also champions. One of his famous sons was Ch. Harmony of Ttiweh, who went to Holland to Mme Van den Boom to help re-found the breed over there.

Another very famous dog in this breed is the Tricolour Ch. Aloysius of Sunninghill owned by Miss P. Turle. He won nineteen C.C.s and has had ten champion offspring, including Mr Campbell Martin's S. African Ch. Marrakesh's Melchior of Kormar and Frau B. Östergren's Int. Ch. Allegra of Sunninghill in Sweden. I think it is true to say that these two dogs have had a greater influence on the breed than any other dog except Ann's Son.

There are now ten Specialist Clubs in England and Scotland. The oldest one, apart from the parent Club, is the Three Counties Pekingese and Cavalier Society. This was formed in 1946 and held a breed show that year. Although there had been the odd class put on for Cavaliers at Championship and other shows, this was the first breed show to be held. Mrs Pitt was the judge and Miss Mayhew's Avril of Astondowns, a Ruby, was Best Bitch and The Young Pretender of Grenewich was Best Dog. These two Clubs remained the only two until the 1960s, when firstly Mrs Keswick formed the Scottish Cavalier Club, and then Mrs Murray and Mrs Burroughs formed the West of England Cavalier Club.

In 1969 the late Miss B. M. Palfree formed the Northern

Cavalier King Charles Society. Apart from the Three Counties Pekingese and Cavalier Society, all the other three Clubs hold championship status and the Northern Society gained this in 1973. The Eastern Counties C.K.C.S. Society was formed in 1976 under the auspices of Mr R. T. G. Ford. Mrs V. Barwell is the Chairman and I think it will be a thriving club in 'the bulge', as Norfolk and Suffolk are known. The Midland Counties Club, with Mrs B. Spencer as Chairman, was founded mainly to bridge the gap between the areas of the West of England Club and the Northern Cavalier Club. We now have a very thriving Southern Club, of which Miss Betty Miller of the 'Otterholt' Cavaliers is the President and I have the honour of being its Patron.

This Club, like all the others, has really worked hard and they have now gained their Championship status. In fact the first Championship Show was held in 1982 and was a great success. We also now have the recently formed South and West Wales Cavalier King Charles Spaniel Club, which I am sure will be of great help to owners of Cavaliers in that part of the country. The most important thing in our breed today is to find the right homes for our puppies. Whether or not they are for show does not matter, they must go to people who care about their dogs. Only too frequently do we hear of far too young puppies being found in pet shops in London as well as other places.

During the Second World War the breeding of Cavaliers had perforce to be drastically reduced. One dog that was used a lot and has certainly left his mark was the Ruby, Cannonhill Richey. He was the sire of Daywell Roger and also of the first Black/Tan dog Champion Mrs V. Rennie's Ch. Royalist of Veren and of many others. His name will be found in a great number of pedigrees.

One of the problems that the original band of breeders had to contend with was bad mouths. This was inevitable, seeing that the 'Charlie' had a very short upturned jaw. These will still appear nowadays, as it is not possible completely to obliterate such a feature in as short a time as the breed has been in existence, but on the whole there are few bad mouths to be found in the show ring today.

In 1964 the first Year Book of the Club was produced. A lot of hard work was put into this and all the credit goes to Colonel (now Brigadier) Jack and Mrs Burgess. This was a much needed publication and with the Club's membership now so large, was entirely warranted. The Scottish Club followed suit in 1965 with a most helpful Year Book, and also in that year Foyle's produced one of their excellent handbooks on Cavaliers written by Mrs Stenning.

At Championship Shows Cavaliers have been well to the fore with top honours. Among them was Mrs Keswick's Ch. Pargeter Bob Up, who was Best Toy at Richmond some years ago, and her Ch. Pargeter Anemone was also Best Toy at Birmingham National in 1959. Ch. Pargeter Melissa was Best Toy at the L.K.A. in 1962 and Mr V. Bennett's Ch. White Collar Worker was Best Toy at Blackpool in 1960. One win of long ago which cannot be omitted, as it was a great boost for the breed, was Ch. Harmony of Ttiweh's Best in Show win at the South Eastern Toy Dog Show. Although not a Championship Show, all the other Toy Breeds had their champions there, including Pekes, and when Mr Fullwood awarded the Best in Show to a Cavalier, which was the first time ever, it was really like piercing the Iron Curtain.

Another Birmingham National win was Mrs Pitt's Ch. Polka of Ttiweh, who was Best Bitch there on the first day, and in 1966 her Sugar Crisp of Ttiweh was Best Dog on the first day at the Three Counties. Birmingham seems to be lucky for Cavaliers. In 1958 Miss Turle's Ch. Aloysius of Sunninghill was Best Toy Dog and also in the same year he repeated that feat at the L.K.A. My own Ch. My Fair Lady of Eyeworth was Best Member's Bitch in Show both days at the W.E.L.K.S. in 1959 and later on in 1963 Ch. Mimi of Eyeworth was Reserve Best Member's Bitch the first day at the same show. Mrs Cryer had the joy and pride of handling Ch. Amelia of Laguna to become Best Toy at Cruft's in 1963 and another top honour was my Ch. Discus of Eyeworth, who was Reserve Best Toy at Richmond in 1965. Mrs Keswick's Ch. Pargeter Myrrhis was Best Toy at Belfast in 1966 under Mr Siggers and Reserve Best in Show under Mr Fenton Fitzgerald. Ch. Pargeter McBounce won the Toy Group at Windsor in 1966. Ch. Cherrycourt

Wake Robin won the Toy Group at the City of Birmingham in 1967, and in 1968 Ch. Bowstones Victoria of Littlebreach was runner up in the Toy Group at Windsor under Mr Alva Rosenberg. My own Ch. Archie McMuck of Eyeworth won the Toy Group at Dumfries in 1969 and three Reserve Toy Groups as well as being Best Puppy in Show of all breeds at Bath in 1968, and Best Members' Dog in Show both days at the W.E.L.K.S. in 1970.

We now have thirty-two sets of Certificates on offer, which means that we have C.C.'s in all the General Championship Shows, the United Kingdom Toy Dog Society and the Breeds Clubs as already stated.

There is no doubt that a lot of the popularity of the breed is due to the fact that many spaniel lovers have moved into smaller houses and want a smaller spaniel, and a number of Cocker owners have changed to Cavaliers for this very reason and are delighted with their new breed. This has happened all over the world and the parent club has members from all the countries where there are Cavaliers.

Watching round the ringside when judging is going on, it is most encouraging to see how much more uniform the breed has become. The all-rounders particularly stress this point and a lot of them have known Cavaliers for a long time. They have become smaller and are what the Standard set them out to be. Naturally you get the odd very large one cropping up and also the very tiny ones, but this is the exception rather than the rule.

Cavaliers have appeared in films and on television and everywhere they go they are admired and loved. Her Royal Highness Princess Margaret had a very loved one called Rowley and he was always in great evidence in photographs taken at home.

Unfortunately with the recent large increase of exhibitors and breeders and the popularity of Cavaliers, the breed has become much more commercial and the cost of puppies has gone up enormously. The cost of showing has also gone up by a great amount, so this necessitates a rather different outlook on the scene and the breed is no longer a small, happy band of people working for the good of the Cavalier. This always happens when a breed becomes too big – and it is sad to see it happening to ours. There are still quite a few of the older breeders who try their best to keep the breed as it should be. It would not be fair only to mention a few names of breeders who have done much for the breed and been very successful, but in Appendix C can be found all the champions that have ever been in the breed in England, together with their colour, the names of their sires and dams, owners, breeders and date of birth. From that the reader can deduce for himself who has been and is most prominent in the breed.

A great achievement in the breed in recent years is the making of many Ruby champions in this country and judges have come to recognize that their conformation is now just as good as any other of the colours, and they have the same flashiness. It is still true to say that the whole colours have a harder time to reach the top but the great thing is that they have made it.

There have been ten Black and Tan champions in this country. One of the reasons for the improvement in Black and Tans is that by mating them with the parti-colours much of the old curly coat of the Truffle dog has been bred out and they now have sleek shining black coats.

The Cavalier today has certainly 'arrived'. At many Championship Shows now Cavaliers are in the last line-up for Best in Show, and they are regularly the top Toy Breed entry. There are many newcomers to be seen in the ring, but personally I would like them to know a little more of the breed rather than attempting to absorb everything in five minutes. I am sure that Mr Roswell Eldridge must be happy looking down from his cloud, but is he right? I know I am not alone in this thought that the breed is not going from strength to strength in the way that Mrs Pitt and her band of pioneers started. If we don't take care we shall destroy that image and produce small, light-eyed dogs with snipey noses, bad construction and heavily marked Blenheims and Tricolours, but I'm sure that Mr Roswell Eldridge must have taken great pride in Messrs Hall and Evans' Ch. Alansmere Aquarius winning Supreme Best in Show at Cruft's in 1973, going round the ring looking every inch a 'Royal'.

3

The Standard

IT IS only since the advent of Kennel Clubs all over the world that Breed Standards have come into being. Before that it was really what the so-called individual experts of those days considered was correct that was accepted.

Our own Kennel Club was founded in 1873, but owing to the Victorian King Charles with the domed head, which had become fashionable, our Cavalier Standard was not drawn up until the formation of the Club. The drawing up of the Standard took place on the second day of Cruft's in 1928 when the first Club Meeting was held, and has been very little altered since then. The line pattern was Miss Mostyn Walker's Ann's Son. Various members brought along reproductions of the paintings of the sixteenth, seventeenth, and eighteenth centuries where the Toy Spaniels were portrayed, and from all this emerged the Standard. A Standard is not a rigid formula in which every point must be conformed with, this obviously would be quite impossible, for to do this the perfect dog must be produced and that is something that will never happen. No, it is a pattern to aim for (especially in our very early days) to make a uniformity in the breed, especially with regard to size.

We will now enumerate the points and then study them in greater detail. By kind permission of the Kennel Club we reproduce the Standard of Points.

General appearance. An active, graceful, well-balanced dog. Absolutely fearless and sporting in character and very gay and free in action. Totally free from trimming and all artificial colouring.

Head and skull. Head almost flat between the ears without dome. Stop shallow; length from base of stop to tip about one and a half inches. Nostrils should be well developed and the pigment black. Muzzle well tapered. Lips well covering but not hound-like. Face should be well filled out underneath the eyes. Any tendency to appear 'snipey' is undesirable.

Eyes. Large, dark and round, but not prominent. The eyes should be well spaced apart.

Ears. Long and set high, with plenty of feathering.

Mouth. Level. Scissor bite preferred.

Neck. Moderate length, slightly arched.

Forequarters. Shoulders well laid back.

Legs. Moderate bone and straight.

Body. Should be short-coupled with plenty of spring of rib. Back level. Chest moderate, leaving ample heart room.

Hindquarters. Legs – moderate bone, straight.

Feet. Compact and well cushioned.

Coat. Long, silky and free from curl. A slight wave is permissible. There should be plenty of feather.

Tail. The docking of tails is optional. The length of the tail should be in balance with the body.

Colour – The only recognized colours are:

Black and Tan. Raven black with tan markings above eyes, on cheeks, inside ears, on chest and legs and underside of tail. Tan should be bright.

Ruby. Whole coloured rich red.

Blenheim. Rich chestnut marking well broken up on a pearly white ground. The markings should be evenly divided on the head, leaving room between the ears for the much valued lozenge mark or spot (a unique characteristic of the breed).

Tricolour. Black and white, well spaced and broken up, with tan markings over the eyes, on cheeks, inside ears, inside legs and on underside of tail. Any other colour or combination of colours is most undesirable.

Weight and size. Weight twelve to eighteen pounds. A small well-balanced dog, well between these weights, is desirable.

Faults. Light eyes. Undershot and crooked mouths and pig jaws. White marks on whole-coloured specimens. Coarse-ness of type. Putty noses. Flesh marks. Nervousness.

Note. Male animals should have two apparently normal testicles fully descended into the scrotum.

As will be noticed there is no mention at all of any trimming anywhere. This was done purposely with the hope that the Cavalier would remain a perfectly natural dog, guarded from fashion and not liable to be spoilt by individual flights of fancy with regard to its shape.

Head and skull can best be explained by looking at the following drawings. The great point of the King Charles is the massive domed skull, which is entirely wrong for a Cavalier.

Eyes. Should be a dark liquid brown, not black. They must be spaced well apart to give the gentle expression which is so much a characteristic of a Cavalier. Closely set eyes will give a hard, mean expression. There should almost be pouches under the eyes which give the illusion that the eyes are

Figure 1   Correct head
Correct head. Shallow
stop

Incorrect head. Domed skull
Incorrect head. Deep stop, short
muzzle

Thomas Fall

Ch. Dickon of Little Breach (Blenheim)

C. M. Cooke

Ch. Cantella of Eyeworth (Tricolour)

Detail from
La Toilette
by Antoine
Watteau
(1684–1721)

Anne's Son
(Blenheim)

Right
Ch. Daywell Roger
(Blenheim)

Below
Ch. Raoul of Ttiweh
(Blenheim)

Portrait Group of Three Children by Sofonisba Anguisciola (*c.* 1535–1626)
A. C. Cooper (by permission of the Lord Methuen, R.A., 4th Baron)

St James's Park by George Morland (1763–1804)
L. H. Hill (by permission of Her Grace the late Constance Duchess of Westminster, D.B.E.)

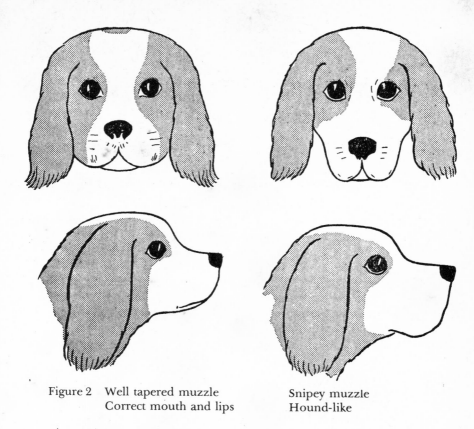

Figure 2   Well tapered muzzle   Snipey muzzle
            Correct mouth and lips   Hound-like

prominent, when in fact they are not. A small eye is very often aligned to a too-pointed nose, giving a fox-like face.

Ears. Should be as shown in the diagram of a correct Cavalier head. (Figure 1)

Mouth. The teeth in this should consist of sixteen pre-molars, ten molars, four canines and twelve incisors. They should be level all the way round, with the top front teeth just closing over the bottom front teeth, forming what is called a 'scissor bite'. (Figure 4)

Any fault in the construction of the mouth – i.e. undershot or overshot mouths – will give a faulty bite and may make eating difficult. The very overshot mouth is termed a 'parrot mouth' and is generally seen more in horses than in dogs. It is

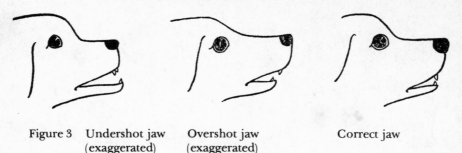

Figure 3   Undershot jaw   Overshot jaw   Correct jaw
                (exaggerated)   (exaggerated)

seldom seen in a Cavalier, but the odd one does crop up and is as much a fault as an undershot jaw. (Figure 3)

Another bad fault is a wry mouth. This is when the jaw itself is wrongly shaped. Teeth growing at odd angles is also a fault; it is generally the canines that do this, but the incisors also can be ragged and uneven.

An undershot mouth can very easily come right by a year old, but a parrot mouth never becomes right.

Neck. Is dealt with in the next chapter, as are the next four items, *Forequarters, Legs, Body* and *Hindquarters*.

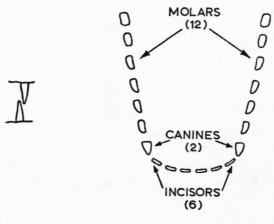

Figure 4   Scissor-bite teeth   Teeth in upper jaw
                                            Lower jaw is similar,
                                            but has 14 molars

Coat. The Cavalier coat is definitely not of such a silky texture as that of the 'Charlie' and this is to be lamented. Nothing looks or feels more beautiful than a silky coat. A slight wave is rather pretty, but a very curly coat spoils the shape of the dog. Cavaliers are very apt to go curly with old age.

Tail. If this is docked, one-third should be taken off.

Colour. The Black and Tan should have no white on it at all; very frequently at birth, and while a youngster and unfeathered, there will be a little patch of white on the chest, but this will disappear when the featherings come in. There must be no white on the head. The same applies to the Ruby – a small fleck of white on a Ruby's head will almost certainly be gone by about seven or eight months, but a larger blaze probably won't go. These two colours are known as whole colours. Blenheims and Tricolours should be well broken up, although there are many heavily marked champions in both these colours. It would be wrong to down-grade an otherwise excellent dog in the show ring just on this technicality. This may be said of the Black and Tans and Rubies, but to allow either of these to win if they have white on would be wrong. The word 'whole' colour would have lost its meaning and they would virtually be parti-coloured, which is what Blenheims and Tricolours are called.

Here might be said a word about colour in breeding. No matter what parti-colour genes are in a dog, if Blenheim is mated to Blenheim it will always produce Blenheims. They are completely dominant together. A Blenheim and Tricolour mating may produce both colours, or you can get a litter of either one or the other. Tricolour mated to Tricolour will also produce both colours, but very often the Tricolours will be more broken up than the ones out of a Blenheim and Tricolour mating.

So much for the parti-colours mating together. The whole colours present rather a different outlook. The Ruby is the least dominant of all the colours and therefore the most difficult to breed true. A Ruby mated to a Black/Tan is a very good mating. Provided the Black/Tan or Ruby is a dominant, there will only be whole colours in the litter – if neither parent is dominant all four colours can be produced. Ruby to Ruby, if one parent is a dominant, will produce all Rubies, but if not,

Blenheims can appear and will generally have a rich colour. Black/Tan to Black/Tan can produce all four colours, again if the parents are not dominant.

The mating of the parti-colours to the whole colours is not really a very good idea, as so many mismarked Rubies and Black/Tans can be produced. There are, naturally, exceptions to every rule and many good Black/Tans have been produced in this way.

If a Blenheim or Tricolour is mated to a dominant Black/Tan only whole colours will be in the litter, but they are quite likely to be mismarked. If the Black/Tan is not dominant, then all four colours may be the result, and the same applies to a Tricolour mating with Ruby or Black/Tan.

The greatest of the early experts on genes and chromosomes was undoubtedly Dr Gregor Mendel, who lived from 1822 to 1884. His researches are so well known that they are known as Mendelism, and any reader who wishes to delve more deeply into the colour hereditary factor would be well advised to read his book.

Weight and size. This is probably the thing that puzzles most novices. A Cavalier has fairly heavy bone and even a fairly small dog can weigh fifteen pounds. Conversely, a tall lightly boned dog may weigh less. Cavaliers are classified as Toys, therefore they must not look like Welsh Springer Spaniels. They must be in proportion, with the short coupled back and the length of the leg which is right for the balance of the dog. They must not be weedy, and there are very few Cavaliers even of ten pounds who do not look weedy. Only by experience and a good eye for a dog can this puzzling question be sorted out. It is true today that looking at a class of Cavaliers in the show ring they are seen to be very much more uniform now than they used to be, although the really good ones of yesteryear were the same as the first-class specimens are today.

Faults. Light eyes – this is a very bad fault and hard to breed out. They will alter the whole expression of the face and have much the same effect as small eyes, giving a hard expression.

Undershot and crooked mouths we have already dealt with – an overshot mouth or parrot mouth is just as much a fault and can be very unsightly, also they affect digestion as mastication cannot take place properly.

Coarseness of type is largely caused by a short neck and very heavy bone. A large dog, even though far too big for the Standard, need not be coarse. Putty noses are difficult things to deal with. Many solutions have been put forward but none have found the answer. The most general thought is that it is a hormone deficiency. A bitch will have an off-colour nose just before and during her season, but will have a jet-black one after a litter of puppies. A dog with a pink nose is a much more acute problem. Whilst a bitch with a slightly off-coloured nose may be partly forgiven, a dog with one must be penalized in the show ring. A flesh mark on the nose is known as a 'butterfly nose' and although it is classified as a fault, provided it is not too large and the other qualities of the dog are excellent I doubt if it would have too much effect on its career in the show ring. It is also preferable not to have a brown smudge on one side of the lip, although this again should not be penalized too heavily. Nervousness is a serious fault and should be penalized. It is hereditary, unless caused by a bad shock in youth, and detracts seriously from a gay, active, fearless dog which the General Appearance says we are aiming at.

Apart from the formation of the jaw, the whole of the structure of the Cavalier has been left until the next chapter.

4

Conformation and Characteristics

IN THE previous chapter we read what the Standard is and how it should be translated, but now those translations must go a little further into the conformation of a dog. All animals including humans have the same kind of mechanical structure, such as ribs, spine, tibia, fibula and femur bones, ball and socket joints, etc. To get an overall picture it is necessary to understand the correct positioning of all these bones and joints, why they are there and what use they are.

The term 'a sound dog' means that each of these parts is correctly placed and each one is playing its part. No matter how well the brain sends its messages to the various parts of the body these parts cannot function properly if they are out of place. The brain sends its messages to the muscle fibres which clothe the skeleton as a whole and are attached to the bones and joints. There is a central nervous system which sends its messages by a highly complex method of electric impulses. If it can be thought of rather to resemble a big radio transmitting station perhaps some idea may be had of how complex it is. This system is controlled either consciously or subconsciously by the will and must not be confused with the involuntary system which maintains throughout life the functioning of the body, such as respiration, blood circulation, digestion, the conception and bearing of puppies, and all those other changes, mainly hormone, which go on during the course of a lifetime. This system can be affected by the nervous one but not controlled by it.

The Cavalier should be a sound little dog of medium bone. It should also be elegant and full of glamour as well as being gay. The chest should not be too narrow and the ribs should have a good spring to them. Nothing is more unattractive than a slab-sided Cavalier. The neck should have a good reach to it, which means that the shoulder must be well laid back and not

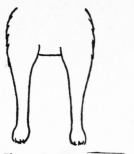

Figure 5 Good front and good feet

Front too narrow Splayed feet

Front too wide Turned in toe Out at elbow

upright. Failure to possess this makes the dog look very short-necked and unattractive.

Apart from looking unattractive it may also hamper his work in the field and Cavaliers do make excellent retrievers for small game. A dog with a good reach of neck can pick up running almost at any speed, whereas a short or bull-necked dog, unless it stops almost dead, will fall over itself as it stoops to retrieve.

The legs should be straight-boned, nicely feathered, with the elbows set in well to the body. An elbow that sticks out either when standing or walking is a fault and is also very ugly. The feet should be well up on the pasterns, not as high as a hound, but they must have strength in them. They should be compact and feathered. The entire front of a Cavalier should be symmetrical, and the feet should not be splayed or turned in.

The body should be short-coupled. A longer back is sometimes permitted in a bitch for breeding purposes, but in a dog is very ugly.

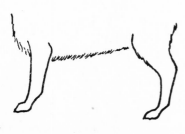

Figure 6 Good pasterns

Weak pasterns

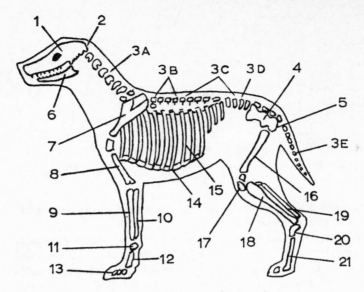

Figure 7   Skeleton of a Cavalier

1.	Skull	5.	Pelvis	14.	Sternum
2.	Occiput	6.	Jawbone	15.	Ribs
3.	Vertebrae	7.	Scapula	16.	Femur
	A 7 Cervical	8.	Humerus	17.	Patella
	B 4 Dorsal	9.	Radius	18.	Tibia
	C 5 Lumbar	10.	Ulna	19.	Fibula
	D 6 Sacral	11.	Carpus	20.	Tarsus
	E Tail (undocked)	12.	Metacarpus	21.	Metatarsus
4.	Ilium	13.	Phalanges		

The Rib Cage

From the diagram it can be seen that there are thirteen bones on either side which form this cage. These should be well rounded to give the spring of rib already mentioned. Slab-sidedness is when these bones are not sufficiently curved. On the top of this cage runs the spine which consists of twenty-five vertebrae containing the spinal cord. They are divided in the anatomical sense into three parts. The first seven, which are above the scapula, are called the cervical group and support the neck. The next group, which contains the thirteen pairs of ribs, is called the dorsal or thoracic. These embody the heart, lungs and chest, and should they not be rounded enough, will not give sufficient space for these organs to function properly. The lumbar group, which is in the loin region, contains five vertebrae and is located where humans get lumbago.

Behind these three groups lies a solid bone called the sacrum. This is made from fused vertebrae and forms the upper side of the pelvis which is then followed by the tail vertebrae. The pelvis structure is one of the most important and should it be deformed, either at birth, or by an accident, may prevent natural whelping. If it doesn't actually prevent natural whelping it will make it very difficult.

Figure 8   Well turned stifle   Straight stifle

The hindquarters should be nicely angulated with the femur bone fitting well with the tibia by means of the patella. This is a ball-and-socket joint and is the one that is most likely to slip. An operation can be performed to pin the bones, but as it can very easily be hereditary it is extremely unwise to have this done and no dog or bitch with a slipping patella should be

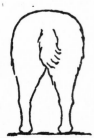  

Figure 9   Correct hind legs   Cow-hocked   Bow-hocked

Figure 10   Correct back and   Dipped back and
               tail carriage   gay tail

used for breeding. Too straight a stifle in a Cavalier is often a cause for a slipping patella.

The back legs, when seen from behind, should be straight down to the hock, which will then slope under in a straight line. A leg which turns outwards from the hock or inwards is wrong.

The back of a Cavalier, from the top of the scapula or shoulder-blade, should be straight, with the tail rounding off the pelvis and lying naturally between the hind legs. When feathering or working in the field this tail should work from side to side. A gay tail carried at an angle above the body is ugly, especially when undocked. A dipping back may produce this, or if the tail is set on too high.

Cavaliers are great water dogs and for this reason are used especially in America for dove and quail shooting. They can go through brambles easily and are strong swimmers. They have good mouths and noses and will give tongue in true spaniel fashion.

Some are more sporting-minded than others, and the ones that are become quite oblivious to any calling or whistling when really on the go. Naturally the ones that are trained to the gun should obey the handler's commands.

One great characteristic of the breed is snorting – somewhat like a choking cough. This may easily be stopped by placing the hand over the nose for a few seconds. Another trait of theirs is to love to lie on a low stool with one front paw tucked under and the other lying along the top of the stool. They look very royal in this position and one can imagine them looking like this on a satin cushion in the days of King Charles.

They are very loyal and constant companions and like to be with their owners all the time. They even prefer to sit in the car all day, rather than be left at home. They are highly intelligent and their IQ by canine standards is quite high. They are adaptable – indeed so well do they adapt themselves to human life that one might well think that they have a near-human mentality. Much as one would like this to be the case, it is, of course, an impossibility. Many of their senses are much more strongly developed than ours – smell and hearing for instance – but the mental processes are on quite a different plane. This makes a complete mutual understanding impossible, but as far as they can a Cavalier will understand its owner and certainly they can assimilate their fears and joys. A highly nervous person will generally end up with a highly nervous Cavalier, and vice-versa – a very boisterous person will have a boisterous Cavalier. This idiosyncrasy is to be noticed very much in the whelping bitch. If the owner is hysterical the bitch will be too. If the owner is practical it's far more likely that the bitch will be also. They have great faith in their owner and are not at all an independent breed, except when hunting, and then they revert to a pack with a single leader, as they would have been before man controlled them.

It is interesting to note the behaviour of the Cavaliers on the show benches. As a rule they are lying quietly, probably asleep. There are, of course, exceptions to every rule and indeed noisy ones are to be found, but it is generally because they are allowed to be noisy, for they do not bark like many other toy dogs do. One more reason for choosing a Cavalier!

5

Choosing a Puppy

HAVING read thus far, it is presumed that the new enthusiast
has really made up his mind that a Cavalier is quite definitely
the breed for him. Now arises the question from where to get a
puppy, or it may be a more adult dog that is wanted. In either
case it is hoped that the advice that follows will be of use to the
potential owner.

If possible, it is most helpful to attend one or more of the big
Championship Shows where Cavaliers can be seen in quantity
and quality. The majority of breeders will be at these shows
and if a puppy is wanted for definite show purposes, it is
usually true to say that the most successful in the show ring will
have the best stock. As they are known for the quality they
produce it would not be worth their reputations as well-known
breeders to sell either bad quality or unhealthy stock. This in
no way detracts from the smaller breeder with perhaps a
couple of good brood bitches who produce excellent stock,
but it is most advantageous for the novice to see the quality of
the stock that a kennel is producing.

Cavaliers alter very much indeed as they mature and no one
who has any knowledge at all of the breed will guarantee that
an eight-week-old puppy will definitely turn out to be a big
winner. For one thing, mouths can alter up to two years and
the mouth of a young puppy can go either way. It is rare for a
mouth to go wrong once the second teeth are through, which
should be at about three months old, but a slightly undershot
mouth can very easily come right. This is due to the fact that
the nose, which when born is very snub and has a bump on the
top, will continue to get longer through maturity, thus
bringing forward the top jaw. It is true to say that the larger the
bump, the longer the nose will eventually become. It is also
possible that a puppy who actually looks undershot – that is

with the lower jaw protruding – will also end up with a perfect mouth, but this is more unlikely and I would not recommend a novice to buy a seven- or eight-week old puppy who looks like this.

The reputable breeders will always help the novice in every possible way and as they know so much of the parents' antecedents it is wise to be advised by them. It is of great interest not only to the novice but to all breeders if the colours of the puppy's ancestors can be put on the pedigree, and most of the big breeders will know many if not all of the colours of the ancestors. This is of particular value when the time comes for mating the puppy and it can be seen how much whole colour or parti-colour there is in the pedigree.

Obviously the best way to buy a puppy is to go to the kennel and see the stock on home ground. It will probably be possible to see the parents and grandparents, so that some idea may be had of what the finished product will be like.

Cavaliers do not like being kennel dogs and their individuality will come out to a much greater degree when they become part of a family. They are a loving breed and like to be an intrinsic part of a family.

If the idea is to breed as well as show it is best to start with a bitch puppy. There will be plenty of stud dogs to whom the bitch can go when the time comes, and it is a much more rewarding feeling eventually to win with something that is home-bred.

The idea of going to Championship Shows is to give novices a chance of starting to get their eye in, so that they have some idea of what they are looking for. Also they can decide which colour they prefer, and again by going to the shows they can discover which breeder has the better kennel for the colour wanted.

What to look for
A good cobby body is one of the first things to look for, with not too much heavy bone, although even this can be misleading, as many Cavaliers make all their growth in their early months and then stay static; conversely they may be late starters and suddenly shoot up, possibly becoming rangy and

ill-balanced. This is all the luck of the game, and must be treated as such. It is no good coming back on the breeder at this stage, for he or she will have sold in good faith and only said what they thought would happen.

Light eyes will never become dark and as this is a bad fault should obviously be avoided. By light eyes I mean anything that shows the slightest sign of a yellowy tinge. Some puppies' eyes at an early age still have the rather blue colour of the newly born, rather as a human baby always has blue eyes when first born and it is not always possible to tell definitely what colour they are going to finish up, and this will probably not become apparent until about three months old.

Small umbilical hernias are fairly frequent and should not cause any distress later on; neither will they be unsightly, as the long coat will cover this, but a hernia in the groin is a different matter. It may right itself, but equally it may have to be operated on and it should be carefully watched for fear of strangulation of the intestines. The veterinary surgeon should see it about once a month to assess whether or not an operation will be necessary.

High-set ears, which produce what is termed 'a flat head', are another point. Obviously no head can be completely flat and it is the placing of the ears which gives this illusion and is such a feature of the good Cavalier. Certainly a puppy's ears will come up with maturity, but to be on the safe side it is advisable, anyway for the novice, to start off with a miniature of the finished product.

Small eyes should also be avoided. In another chapter the whys and wherefores of this have been gone into, so it is sufficient to say that even though the eye will enlarge with the growth of the animal it is wiser to start with the more perfect specimen.

Pigmentation will change greatly as the puppy matures, especially in the case of the Blenheims. Quite often they are born with hardly any brown markings to be seen at all, but these will appear by three or four weeks and darken as the puppy grows older.

The skin should be soft and supple with a good sheen on it and possibly a slight wave in the coat. Occasionally a young puppy will have a 'teddy-bear' coat, but this will come out around the time that the second teeth are coming through.

The stifles should be well turned, so that when the puppy walks it picks its hind legs up under him with a good drive. This is most important, as a straight-stifled Cavalier can never move in the way that Nature intended it to do.

Temperament is a very important feature, but it is sometimes more difficult to assess in this breed owing to the fact of the kennel-bred puppy changing its character on becoming a house dog, but it is true to say that a gay and lively little person will remain like it, whilst a very highly nervous type is unlikely to become a good show dog. Obviously bad handling, cruelty, or neglect will bring about a bad temperament which is not an hereditary factor and this can be gauged by the behaviour of the parents of the puppy and the other inmates of the kennel. It is very essential to gain the confidence of a puppy at once as harsh methods never work on any animal, although firmness must be employed in the initial training.

The tail. The prospective buyer must make up his mind whether he wants a docked or undocked puppy. The length of the tail varies in each individual dog and some may have a relatively short tail for an undocked puppy whilst another one may have a very long one, which if carried very high (the technical term is 'gay') will come right up over the back and look ugly. As far as the Standard is concerned, either docked or undocked is quite correct. If it is docked it should be done at four to five days old when one-third is taken off. In the case of a Tricolour, if possible, a white tip should be left at the end of the tail, as it is more attractive than an entirely black tail. It is always possible to dock a puppy's tail at a much later date, but this must be done by a veterinary surgeon under an anaesthetic.

The new puppy will miss its companions at first and need a lot of tender loving care. A good warm bed is essential with a woolly rug into which it can snuggle and make it its 'home'. A puppy rarely fouls its own bed, so the new owner should not fear too much that the blanket or rug will become unpleasant, and it does make such a difference to the comfort of the new arrival. The next stages in the puppy's life and its training follow in the next chapter.

6

General Management

WHEN considering the management of a dog or dogs two things should be foremost in the mind – food and warmth. These two things are essential for the well-being and growth of an animal, as indeed they are for humans.

A great deal of feeding is largely a question of common sense, but knowledge of why certain things are good and other things bad is very necessary.

Firstly, food should be a balanced diet of protein, carbohydrates and fats, with, if necessary, added vitamins and minerals, including the very small amounts of 'trace elements' that are needed to make the body function properly. The body could be looked upon as a very well-designed machine with every part needing to be kept well oiled and greased to play its part in the general running of the machine. Thus if one part is not functioning 100 per cent this will 'throw out' the workings of the other parts.

Broadly speaking, the sources of protein are vegetables, meat, fish and eggs; the carbohydrates are sugar, bread, potatoes, rice, etc., and the fats are oil, butter, cheese (Cheddar in particular), herrings and milk. The latter contains fat, protein and carbohydrates, and that is the reason why it is so essential in any human or animal diet, particularly when young. The body breaks down these materials by a chemical process so that they may either be utilized at once or stored until needed, such as glucose, which is the most easily digested sugar and is converted into glycogen and stored in the liver.

Vitamins as we know them today were unknown in the olden days and one of the reasons why rickets were so prevalent in both humans and animals was that insufficient fish oils, butter and eggs were eaten. This was probably due to lack of money, for these commodities were too expensive for the poorer people to be able to afford.

Necessary fats are found in vitamin D, which was only discovered in 1915. With so much tinned and dehydrated food on the market today, certain natural vitamins tend to be taken out of the food, therefore they must be replaced by synthetic ones as they are essential to a healthy growth. Vitamin D, as well as preventing rickets, is most necessary for forming strong (not heavy) bone and good teeth. That is why every puppy must have sunlight, which is a natural source of this vitamin. Very often puppies at birth and for some few weeks afterwards are kept under an infra-ray lamp. This is an admirable idea but great care must be taken to wean the puppies slowly from this lamp. It projects vitamin D into the body in larger quantities than a puppy would naturally absorb, therefore if the puppy is suddenly taken away from this artificial source, its own powers of absorbing the vitamin will be considerably reduced and it could then develop rickets.

Alongside vitamin D in importance is vitamin A. It gives resistance to infection and is also a great help to night vision. A lot of experimenting over the latter aid was done during the last war to help the night pilots, and one vegetable which was found to possess a considerable amount of this vitamin was carrots. It is also found in cod-liver and halibut-liver oil, eggs, animal fats and most fresh green vegetables, also tomatoes. Vitamin B is a collection of many substances which are also found in some of the other vitamins. It therefore forms part of a whole and if it is lacking in a diet it will upset the others. It is found naturally in eggs, liver and wheatgerm to name but a few. A yeast preparation such as Vetzyme contains some of the substances and is a good conditioner for dogs. There is another preparation called Canoval on the market which is extremely good and contains all vitamins. It is in tablet form and the dogs like them; they are especially good for puppies and bitches in whelp. Vitamin C or ascorbic acid is the vitamin that was always lacking on long sea voyages before the days of refrigeration. It is generally called the anti-scurvy vitamin and is to be found in fresh green vegetables, oranges, lemons and limes. It was the lack of these foods that gave the sailors scurvy.

Vitamin E is very often used in the form of wheatgerm to correct lack of fertility. It helps either bitches not conceiving at all or dissolving the foetus at some period during the pregnancy. It also has a certain use for the heart muscles and is found in green leaves and the germ of cereals.

The minerals used to be found in the earth, but with the advancement of agriculture and use of fertilizers the natural earth has taken on a rather different look and it is advisable to give a balanced preparation. The minerals needed are zinc, cobalt and iodine, iron manganese and other trace elements, also lime and phosphorus. Seaweed is a natural source of iodine and can easily be given either in powder or tablet form. This mineral deficiency is often considered the reason for a pink nose or general lack of pigmentation. The other school of thought considers that a hormone problem is more likely to be the cause. A rusty nail is very often put into drinking water to provide iron, but possibly this is not the most hygienic method of giving iron and there's no proof it works!

A dog in its natural environment would eat all the necessary foods, including bones, skin and all the offal. It would kill its prey and then eat until it had had sufficient. To facilitate the passing of the bones through the exit of the bowel (called the anus) Nature provided an anal gland. When a difficult-shaped bone or too large a bone was being passed this anal gland was pierced by the bone, emitting a jelly-like substance which then facilitated the passage of the bone. Nowadays, when roughage and bones are not eaten so much, this gland is liable to get blocked and should be cleared. It is not a difficult job and if the veterinary surgeon is closely watched on the first few occasions it should be possible for the owner to do it. Failure to have this done causes a great irritation and the dog will drag its bottom along the floor in the same way as if it had worms. Cavaliers seem to suffer quite a lot from this gland, possibly more than the larger type of dog.

Sloppy food should not be given; this is bad for the teeth and will give no roughage. Meat should be the main part of a healthy diet with the addition of some biscuit meal. Those meals made from the natural wheat are preferable to the ones made with the more refined wheatgerm. It used to be said that white bread could cause fits and hysteria in dogs and to a large extent that was true and even for humans dieticians prefer brown bread to white. Too much liver may cause diarrhoea but is admirable in small quantities. The other offal, including tripe and lights, is good, but is not such a nourishing food. Fish is particularly good for young puppies and bitches just after they have whelped. Herrings are the most nutritious and if the centre bone and larger side ones are extracted before cooking should present no problem. They are rich in fish oil, easily digested and therefore excellent for a puppy's stomach and also the rather delicate stomach of the bitch who has whelped. This very important lady should have only light food – eggs, milk, fish, milk food – mainly protein for forty-eight hours after whelping and as much liquid as she wants. A bowl of fresh water should always be within her reach. Goats' milk is very beneficial for puppies, being more easily digested than cows' milk. Many of the larger kennels keep two or three goats expressly for the puppies and in-whelp bitches.

There is always some difference of opinion as to whether raw or hard-boiled eggs should be given to puppies. The white of the egg contains a lot of albumen which is not considered good for the young, but the latest advocates say that provided the white is well broken and mixed with the yolk it is perfectly all right, therefore raw or hard-boiled can be fed.

Feeding and Training

From about three months onward the puppy begins to become an adolescent and will eat much the same food as an adult, but more frequently.

Much of animal feeding in the young resembles the human, consequently little and often is best for a small stomach. At this period the puppy really starts to make growth and it cannot be emphasized too strongly that wholesome nourishing food to sustain the burden of growing is essential. It is the feeding at this period that will affect the whole of its adult life. Some dogs tend to become rangy as the puppy fat disappears. The milk teeth will be coming out and the new ones need the calcium to come in and make strong teeth. Should the milk teeth remain in when the others are through these should be extracted by a veterinary surgeon. They are quite easy to get out as they have no roots. If they are left in they may well spoil the shape of the mouth and make the second teeth crooked, thereby spoiling the show chances of an otherwise good specimen.

Three meals a day should now be partaken of – breakfast, lunch, and dinner. Breakfast is generally some form of cereal and milk. A lot of the baby cereal foods are excellent with either glucose or brown sugar added. Luncheon should be raw or cooked mincemeat mixed with a little meal that has been soaked in gravy. Only sufficient gravy should be used to soften the meal which should absorb all the liquid. Minced meat is advocated by the author to preclude the young hopeful gulping all the meat and leaving the meal. By mincing the meat the two can then easily be mixed together. Dinner is similar to luncheon, or fish may be substituted as one of the meals. The time of feeding is not a hard-and-fast rule as long as regular hours are kept. Generally speaking breakfast is about 8 a.m., luncheon 12 noon, and dinner 5 p.m. A drink of milk and a dog biscuit are much appreciated during the course of the evening. At this age one herring per meal or two ounces of meat should be sufficient mixed with meal.

Appetites vary a great deal. Some Cavaliers are inordinately greedy and some just couldn't care less about food. In the first case the food must be strictly rationed. Too much fat at any age is bad; in early formative years it is bad for the bone formation and in later years it is a strain on the heart. Very often a puppy will go off its food when taken away from its companion, but the appetite should return within a couple of days. Oddly enough a dog will very often eat bits of food from the floor rather than its bowl or plate and if it can be started in this way will most probably continue to eat from its bowl. A couple of days without food will not do any serious damage, but obviously too long is not going to do any good. Pandering to a dog will not pay dividends and there is a wealth of difference in firm but gentle handling and over-devoted giving-in. Again, rather the same as for a baby, the proprietary brands of malt extract are very good for a poor feeder and help to give some of the much needed vitamins. If Canoval is not being used some form of calcium or bonemeal should be given up to six months old. Exercise should be taken in reasonable quantity. If a garden is available the puppy can exercise itself for as long as it wants and will then go fast asleep. If it is to be taken for walks – and walks as walks are not advocated until at least five months old – care should be taken that it doesn't get tired. If over-exercised, the puppy may tend to get long in leg and out at the elbows. It is inadvisable to take it on the road until after its inoculations.

By five months the puppy should be lead and collar trained. Cavaliers seem happier on the whole in a collar rather than a harness, a light round collar or a thin chain being quite sufficient. To accustom the puppy to having something round its neck the easiest and kindest way is to put the collar on every day and leave it for an increasing length of time. After a few days of this the lead may be attached. Some puppies are much easier to lead train than others and will take to it like a duck to water, others fight madly like young bulls. In this latter case just let the lead trail on the ground with no pressure on it, thereby enabling the puppy to become accustomed to the strange feeling of not being free. Gradually bring a little pressure to bear until the puppy is quite under control. It should then be taught to walk at heel, for nothing is worse for owner or dog than a choking animal straining on the lead. This training is quite simple. Use a short lead to begin with and a rolled-up newspaper just to put in front of the puppy's nose every time it tries to strain. The lead should gradually be lengthened until eventually the puppy is walking fully composed and at heel, with no pressure from the lead at all.

The next thing which should be taught is obedience to commands. This is essential from all points of view and could be the means of preventing an accident and possibly loss of life.

Cavaliers are extremely intelligent and readily absorb all that they are taught. Being royal dogs, they like the best of everything and the best satin cushion in the drawing room is obviously much more preferable than a common basket. But no matter how endearing this little trait may be it is not always practicable and the puppy must be taught as it is intended to continue. To lie in its basket or on the floor in front of the fire is one of the first things to learn; or perhaps there may be a special chair on which it will learn that it is allowed to sit. There are some very good collapsible beds on the market; Goddards and Safari are two of the manufacturers, and if the puppy knows that that is its base he will go to it wherever it is put. This can be very useful when away from home.

To come when it is called or whistled is very essential and the puppy must learn to respect and obey its master, and conversely the owner must learn to treat the puppy sensibly, not contradicting his orders the whole time.

Cavaliers are very loving and faithful. As mentioned in Chapter 7, they don't like being kennel dogs and are happiest when with their owner. They are quick to learn and many of them have done very well in obedience classes. They also make good gun dogs for retrieving smaller birds and for this they must learn to obey commands.

House Training

House training is an extremely important factor in the life of the household. As we are now talking of the adolescent puppy – that is of three months and upwards – it is presumed that it will have learnt some elements of cleanliness. As it grows older it will be able to go longer periods of time without urinating, but still it is important to put the youngster out after every meal, at regular intervals, and whenever it wakes up (this is one of the most likely times for a puddle to be made). Newspaper or a box of sawdust can be used *in extremis*, but the former is not really a terribly good idea, as it can be a little aggravating, particularly to the head of the household, who drops his favourite Sunday paper to the floor after luncheon and wakes up to find it has become a puppy's private retiring room! Sawdust has its advantages in wet weather but should be discontinued as the dog grows older or it will make too much mess.

The majority of the house training will fall upon the most patient member of the family. Very few puppies will do what is expected of them if they are just put out and left to their own devices. It is up to the house trainer to stay out with the pupil, making encouraging noises and then giving extravagant praise when the good deed is done. The same procedure should be applied to any older kennel-reared dog, but in these cases it should take only a short while for the idea to sink in, for Cavaliers are a naturally clean breed. A puppy's bowels will probably function three or four times a day, but this will gradually settle down to once or twice a day as it grows older – generally morning and evening.

A dog is more difficult than a bitch and the lifting of the leg in a strange house is practically an unwritten law in the canine world – particularly if any other dog has done it or there is a bitch in the house. This is a problem, but it seems to be a mark of appreciation and is difficult to overcome.

Car Training

Cavaliers love cars and as a rule are good travellers. It is advisable to give a puppy a small capsule of chlorabutol, which can be obtained from a veterinary surgeon, the first few times it travels. A great deal of car sickness is auto-suggestion and if it never has been sick it won't think of it and consequently won't be. There is always the exception to every rule and for a grown adult dog who is persistently car sick one of the proprietary brands, such as Avonmin, given each time of travelling, can prove very successful. It is very necessary from the accident point of view that the puppy or dog should be trained to sit or lie quietly in a car. Jumping backwards and forwards over the driver is a sure way of promoting an accident. It is unwise to feed a young puppy just before a drive, but when they are established travellers it seems to make very little difference to them.

Warmth

Now we come to the second most important point – warmth.

If more than one dog is kept they may easily be kennelled outside and the ideal building for this is brick. This is completely weatherproof and is much safer from the electricity point of view, but is more expensive than a wooden building. It should have some form of heating, and for this the heaters similar to those on a bathroom wall are very good. All switches should be high up on the wall, well out of reach of enquiring noses. Another form of heating is the tubular. This is excellent, but if placed near the floor should have a wire cage covering it completely. Oil stoves are *not* advised.

Next – the bed. To preclude any possible draughts, a good deep box on legs is recommended with the front cut out to make entry easy. This should be filled with either a blanket or wood wool. Straw may be used, but this is very apt to carry parasites such as lice and flies, and once lice get into a kennel they are extremely difficult to get rid of. If the floor has saw-dust scattered on it it makes the cleaning of it much easier and gives a rather pleasant sweet woody smell.

Cavaliers prefer to sleep one on top of each other; therefore, for two or three of them one big box is perfectly adequate. Even if they are given a bed each it is very rare for them not to get into the one. This is probably a throw-back to the pack instinct where they would lie together for warmth.

If there is to be a run attached to the kennel it should be large enough if possible for the dogs really to be able to run in it. The most hygienic base to have is concrete, but if there are any old bricks available these make a very good base and are porous, which enables them to absorb rain water instead of it lying around in puddles. Some grass or earth is very much appreciated by Cavaliers, as they do love digging. If there is a grass or earth part of the run this must be limed once a year to keep it free from disease. This necessitates keeping the dogs off it for at least four days. Another reason for having concrete or brick foundations is that it keeps the dogs' toenails down. Dogs living entirely on soft ground have to have their toenails cut every so often. This is quite a simple job. Take a pair of nail clippers and hold the paw firmly in the left hand. Each nail will have a transparent piece at the end and this part can be cut; as soon as the nail becomes opaque this means that the quick has been reached and should not be cut. Black toenails are more difficult to deal with, but the clearness can be seen if looked for carefully. If the dew claws have been left on, the same method of cutting applies to them. Very often they will curl right back and dig into the leg, particularly with back dew claws. It is for this reason that they are removed at birth.

To return to the run: a chain-link fence of at least five feet should surround it. Many Cavaliers are tremendous jumpers and some even go up the wire like a cat. In the latter case the only way to keep them in is to have a piece of netting at the top of the fence sloping inwards similar to a deer fence. When building the floor or base of the run it is a good idea to have it slightly on the slope, thus enabling the rain water to run off.

In-Season Bitches

For the owner who has only one or two bitches the question of the housing of the in-season bitches doesn't apply so much, but if any dogs are kept then there is a problem. There is a product called Ovoids on the market today and this will stop the bitch being interesting to the dog. Your veterinary surgeon will tell you about this. The 'knickers' for bitches in season are also very good but not very pretty!

Cavaliers as a breed have as few morals as any other breed and possibly fewer than a great many. It is not only a question of keeping the boys away from the girls; the girls will do their best to get to the boys, which means that doors may be scratched and even gnawed and windows merely there out of which to jump. As at this particular time a bitch tends to catch cold more easily, a warm place to live in is essential and one well away from the dogs.

It is miserable to be alone for three weeks and there is no reason why the other bitches should not do a day at a time in 'purdah' being a companion to the one in season. The bitches should be exercised at least three times a day, preferably somewhere where they can with safety be let off the lead. If they are kept in a room in the house it is well to remember that while in this condition they tend to urinate more than usual.

Cavaliers like to keep themselves as clean as possible, but with a heavy discharge, as sometimes happens, this is impossible and newspaper on the floor of the room will help considerably to keep the room clean, and a washable towel or blanket in the bed is better than a cushion. If there is a special 'purdah' house sawdust can be put on the floor to keep it clean.

The house-trained Cavalier is a very clean animal indeed and gets very upset if it has to make a mess through not being let out sufficiently.

Exercising the Adult Cavalier

A Cavalier is prepared to take as much or as little exercise as its owner wants. It must obviously have the basic requirement of a walk or romp in the garden each day, otherwise its insides will get lazy and cease to function. Again the same formula as with human children should be followed. Like a young child it is no good forcing it into the garden with nothing to play with and no one to talk to. It will only get into mischief which will not be its fault at all and then may get punished for it knows not what.

A good solid rubber ball is an excellent form of amusement or a small rubber dumb-bell that has a bell at each end – this can cause hours of amusement. So often one sees a little puppy sitting shivering on a doorstep obviously very cold and miserable; just a few moments of the owner's time to have a romp would make such a difference to this youngster.

Cavaliers are very good with children and for a child to be brought up with animals is basically a very good thing. Great care, however, must be taken that the puppy is not mauled, bear-hugged, and then dropped by the over-appreciative toddler; on the whole, I fear that little boys tend to be more cruel than little girls. A kitten the same age as the puppy often gets on very well with it and they can become life-long friends, but care must be taken when they are introduced, for a kitten's claws are very dangerous things.

Many people take their Cavaliers when riding. I nearly always used to do this and they adored it. They are inclined to be hunting dogs and if there are two together will exercise themselves in the country by running about and 'feathering' – i.e. nose to the ground finding the smells.

Road exercise on a lead, provided the dog doesn't strain on his collar, is extremely good for slack muscles both in front and behind. A horse that is rather slack in his quarters is made to walk over poles, raised about two feet off the ground and at intervals of about six feet, and this necessitates him drawing his legs and stifles up under him and pushing them forward. Although to do this to a dog is impracticable, a good brisk walk on a road will have much the same effect and will help to correct the slightly loose front and lack of drive in the hindquarters. Running behind a bicycle is not to be advocated for many obvious reasons, but a child whose parents own a certain amount of land where traffic doesn't penetrate may find hours of pleasure bicycling, but not too fast, around the estate with the Cavalier. But certainly not bicycling round and round on the lawn; this is almost certain to end in tears and cause destruction, if not to the dog, to the lawn and flower beds.

General Health

Cavaliers are a healthy breed but there are a few basic rules which must be adhered to to make them trouble-free. Being a long-eared dog, with the ears falling over and obscuring the ear-hole, the ears must be cleaned out at least once a week – the dirt and dust from the ear flaps will collect in the ear and if not cleaned will cause canker. A little olive oil on an orange stick, the end of which has been wrapped in cotton wool, will resolve the problem. If cats live in the house or surrounds it is wise to clean the dog's ears every two weeks against mites with a dressing obtainable from the veterinary surgeon. These are largely carried by cats; they cannot be seen with the naked eye and cause tremendous irritation. Just wipe the inside of the ear out and gently insert the cotton-wool end of the orange stick towards the eardrum. This is where the dust and dirt collects. Should a lot of brown stuff come out when this is done, the ear should continue to be cleaned until it is quite clean. Great care must naturally be taken not to insert the orange stick too far into the eardrum; failure to do this could cause the piercing of the eardrum, so to begin with proceed with great care until it has been established just how far it can be inserted.

The eyes are the next thing. Being large and slightly protruding they are apt to get more dust in than others which causes what is known as 'Cavalier tears'. Also the breed are great diggers, which is no help to anyone's eyes. Just keep the eyes wiped with Optrex or boracic whenever they look a little runny. The more serious of their eye complaints is dealt with in the chapter on Sickness in Cavaliers.

Teeth should be cleaned once a week. A child's toothbrush is the best for this, with a small amount of peroxide added to the water. If the water is very hard the teeth may become coated with tartar, in which case they must be scaled by a veterinary surgeon.

Regular grooming is essential; a Mason Pearson brush is very good and a fine-tooth steel comb; mats in the hair should never be allowed to develop, but on the whole Cavaliers do not matt tremendously.

When they have got filthy and soaking wet dry them down well and then leave them to dry and clean themselves; this they always do. When they have done their part the owners can then take over. A chamois leather, or a silk handkerchief, is an excellent way of putting a finishing shine on to a coat, particularly with the whole-colour dogs.

If it is very muddy or snowy weather it may be found that the mud or snow balls between the toes, and this must be removed or may cause eczema. In the summer, if living in the country, it is advisable to brush them with Cooper's Louse Powder* once a week, for being long-coated they are apt to pick up fleas from the grass and the straw and hay. Hayseeds are apt to get between the toes and during the hay period the feet should be watched for this. They also will cause a great irritation and finally eczema.

If these few basic rules are followed a Cavalier should remain a very healthy little dog. There is no necessity for Cavaliers to be bathed frequently unless being shown. Unfortunately they have a great 'penchant' for 'dung heaps' and anything really 'fruity'. It doesn't hurt them in the least to be bathed and a bath every so often is a very good idea, and of course essential after one of these expeditions. Choose a good dog shampoo, see that the water is the right temperature, and dry well. A hand hair-dryer is an excellent way to apply the finishing touches and they do not seem to mind it at all.

---

*An even better preparation is an aerosol called Nuvan Top, but this can be obtained only from a veterinary surgeon or chemist.

To sum up, it is very true to say that kindness plus firmness is the best way of dealing with any dog. The owner must always be the master, but any kind of cruelty will get one nowhere. Animals respond to kindness in the same way as humans do, unless of course you have the 'delinquent child', that is a psychological case, which only an expert can deal with, and in the animal world should this occur, hard though it may seem, it is better to put the animal down.

A Cavalier should be a joy to its owner, and if it is not disciplined it won't be. Therefore, for everyone's well-being, it is better to follow these few simple basic-training hints.

7

Breeding and Puppy Rearing

ONCE the Cavalier enthusiast has reached the stage of owning a fully grown animal the next consideration is whether or not to breed.

Many people consider that to use a dog at stud a few times and then never again will upset them and make them very sexy. This is not at all true and many a young male dog, having been mated, will settle down much more quietly and not be a nuisance to all and sundry. For the owner who is not showing it is a more difficult problem to find a bitch with whom to mate the dog. If a suitable bitch is not known to the owner a letter to the breeder will often be very beneficial. The breeder might even like to use the dog himself or might know of someone who has a bitch of some particular breeding that would match the dog's.

There are three forms of breeding systems – in-breeding, line-breeding and out-breeding.

In-breeding is not recommended to the novice. It entails knowing all the good points and faults in the ancestors and then mating possibly mother to son or father, and daughter to father or son. To do this the progeny must be very carefully culled, for a great many of the genes are going to be fixed by this method. That is to say that the same fault on both sides will become very dominant and equally the same good point will become dominant. Genetics is a most complicated subject and the reader would be advised, if he is really interested in genetics, to read one of the books written by an expert on this subject.

It is sufficient to say here that all animals have certain genes in their make-up; obviously a brother and sister will carry genes more like each other than two animals from two different strains. These genes are passed on by both parents to the offspring causing an hereditary factor. It is for this reason that in-breeding can be a dangerous thing for the novice. In any case it is a long-term policy and may take several years before the ultimate object is realized.

Line-breeding is a modified method of in-breeding. It is breeding to a family or strain but nothing like as close as the mother/son and brother/sister angle. If any particular strain is in the type of animal that is liked it is then advisable to keep to that strain with an occasional out-cross to bring in any particular feature that is considered lacking.

Any indiscriminate breeding with, say, the dog next door is not the way to breed champions. It can obviously succeed, but the more successful breeders choose their stud dogs with great care and attention to what is behind them.

It is not usual to ask a stud fee for an unproven dog. Once he is proved, then one may be asked for, or if the owner of the bitch doesn't want to pay a fee it is quite usual for the owner of the dog to take either the pick of the litter, or anyway a puppy from the litter. This should be arranged at the time of serving the bitch, and should there be only one puppy in the litter, this technically belongs to the owner of the dog unless otherwise specified. From the point of view of the owner of the bitch it is a more satisfying and rewarding feeling to have a litter that is entirely yours, but for financial reasons the other method may have to be used.

The stud dog should be in good health; in hard condition – that is to say, not fat and flabby – and have a good temperament. Also it is far better not to use a dog with an obvious bad fault.

Unfortunately many dogs in many breeds today have been used when they should not have been, and many of the defects which are now becoming apparent need not have happened if a little thought had gone into breeding, and also if puppies hadn't been turned out like sausages from a machine for the pet market. So again the point is stressed that care *must* be taken over breeding. Any reputable breeder is always more than willing to give advice to the novice and as they've probably had years of experience it is wise to take it.

Out-breeding. Out-breeding is sometimes a great success,

sometimes not, and very often doesn't appear to be proving successful until the second or third generation.

Sometimes, for various reasons, it is necessary to try an out-cross. Perhaps some particular point is losing its strength, maybe eyes are becoming smaller or pigment is receding, then an out-cross is advisable to a dog that has the particular points needed. An out-cross is a strain which has virtually nothing to do with your own. The first generation from this crossing is quite often a great failure, but it is worth persevering with after giving thought to the next mating.

General Management of the Stud Dog

In most cases the bitches visit the dogs and are generally left for a couple of nights to acclimatize themselves to the strange surroundings before being mated. This is important to Cavaliers. In some cases the dogs do visit the bitches, but many stud dogs like to perform on their own home ground.

After the bitch has had a night to settle in she should then be introduced to the dog. Provided she is ready for mating – and we'll go into this point later on in the chapter – she will be rather coquettish with him, probably going round him in circles and behaving very much like one is taught to believe Eve behaved to Adam!

This preliminary playing is very essential to the marriage and stimulates the dog to a pitch of great excitement. After a while the dog will try to mount the bitch; she may think she's had enough playing and will then stand, lifting her tail to one side to enable the dog to enter the vagina. In this case it is always advisable to stay at the bitch's head – preferably sitting on a stool for one's own comfort – to steady her should she jerk away at the moment of penetration. If she still wants to go on playing, and the dog is obviously wanting to mate her, then her body should be steadied so that she stands still and again the shoulders should be held to prevent her coming away from him.

When the mating has taken place, and the dog and bitch have tied, the bitch will always begin to lick her lips. Whether or not this is peculiar to Cavaliers the author cannot authoritatively state, but it certainly happens in Cavaliers.

It is wise to put an arm round the rump of the dog and hold

the two together for a short while after the mating has been effected, to ensure a tie. Once this has taken place, the experienced stud dog will turn himself round so that he and the bitch are back to back.

With a young dog he doesn't entirely know what he's done at this moment or what he should then do, and he may collapse on the bitch's back with a forlorn expression on his face, asking for help. When this occurs the two front legs should be gently swung over to one side of the bitch, then the offside hind leg should be put over the bitch's back until they are standing with a reasonable amount of comfort – back to back. All these movements on the human's part must be very quiet and gentle, with soothing words said to both parties about how clever they've been. The tie can last for a few minutes to an hour and if it is an hour quite understandably both parties and the handler get a little bored. It is quite possible and practicable to make the two either sit or lie down. Both rumps should be gently pushed down on to the floor simultaneously and the long wait can then be endured with much greater comfort. A tie is not essential to a mating and some bitches never do tie, but it is considered preferable from the point of view of the owner of the stud dog.

It is *never* advisable to let a dog and bitch mate without supervision. The bitch may be frightened and try to tear herself away from the dog and this could cause untold damage to both. If the bitch is restless she should be firmly held so as not to pull the dog about.

It is always advisable to use a proven dog on a maiden bitch and vice versa; this is merely common sense and not for any reason of genetics or anything like that.

After the two have become separated the bitch should be allowed to rest in her quarters, and the dog, after a very short while, be put back into his quarters. It is most important from the stud dog's point of view that the bitches in season are kept well away from his domain. Failure to do this will cause him great frustration, lack of appetite and, consequently, condition. The culmination of these things will mean that the dog cannot be shown as he looks so poor with the resultant lack of demand for studs.

Any potential breeder likes the sire of the puppies to be well known as a winner in the show ring, if not a champion, and a dog surrounded by bitches in season will not be in show condition.

It is not advisable to use a young dog too often at stud. Start him off at about a year and then let him have perhaps one a month until he is fully matured. This can vary in age, but the average Cavalier is not fully matured until eighteen months old.

The Brood Bitch

The average age for a Cavalier bitch to come into season is nine to ten months; it does happen earlier and also they can go to thirteen months before coming in. The first season is often too early to mate them unless they happen to be very late in season and very mature, then it is permissible.

If the Cavalier owner has become very enthusiastic over breeding and wants to increase the kennel, and possibly cannot afford to buy a good adult brood bitch, it is possible to have a bitch from someone on breeding terms.

These terms can vary quite considerably; if no money passes and the bitch is – we hope – of good quality and breeding, the owner of the bitch may say they want the whole of the first litter and will then transfer the bitch to the new owner, or they may say they want first and third pick of the first litter and second and fourth of the second litter; the stud dog in each case to be named by the owner and the fees paid by the prospective owner, or some money may be exchanged with the proviso that the owner has *a* puppy from the first two litters. Whatever the arrangements are it is essential to register them with the Kennel Club. There are special forms provided for this; both parties sign the forms with all the qualifying remarks clearly set out. One is retained by the owner, one by the prospective owner, and the third by the Kennel Club. For this there is a fee. This agreement is upheld in a court of law and saves endless arguments between the two parties. It must also clearly be stated what the position is when there is only one or perhaps two puppies.

Many big breeders who don't want to keep too many bitches actually in their kennel favour this method, and it can work very well indeed. At the termination of the agreement the bitch is transferred into the name of the new owner, but prior to that the original owner is the technical breeder of the puppies unless otherwise stated.

Having got as far as this and decided on the stud dog, the next question is 'What is the right time for mating?' This is in some ways an enigma. The usual time is the tenth to fourteenth day, but some bitches are much earlier and some later. It is for this reason that the author advocates (if possible) the bitches being brought to the kennel on the tenth day. In any big kennel there are always a number of bitches in 'purdah', and it is by seeing how they behave to each other that the owner knows when is the right time. When the bitches play together and try to mount each other then is the right time to introduce the dog.

Cavaliers as a breed, particularly as they are not kennel dogs, do not like being pitchforked into a mating. Forced matings are not only unkind but seldom result in puppies. If they can relax and be made to feel at home there is a much greater chance of a good mating. This need not always apply to the well-tried matron, but particularly to the young mother. Therefore if it is possible to leave the bitch for a couple of days it is advisable. There is no such thing as a hard and fast rule for mating. It depends entirely upon when the bitch ovulates – this means when the egg is shed from the ovary.

Generally speaking the heat is broken up into three parts. The first nine days is when there is a heavy discharge and when that ceases is generally the right time for mating. The third week is the finishing off period, but, as has been said before, these are by no means hard-and-fast rules. A bitch can go on discharging until almost the end of her season. The vulva should be very swollen when mating time is ripe, but, again, it need not be and she can also be mated on the twenty-third day. Whatever day she is mated on she must be kept shut up for the full three weeks and longer if she still seems flirtatious. One of the old wives' tales is that a bitch will go off heat very soon after mating. This may be so in some cases but should never be relied upon. The only real way of telling is by the bitch's reaction to the dog or other bitches that she is shut up with. It doesn't necessarily follow that each heat will be the same, but it is consistent more often than not.

It is most helpful if the owner of the bitch notifies the stud-dog owner when the bitch has started her season; this enables the owner of the stud dog not to accept bookings around the time that this particular bitch is to be mated.

There are some bitches who will stand right from their first week in season and only by trial and error can you find the right day. If a bitch has missed a couple of times it is a very good thing to mate her from their first day of standing until the end of this period. From the day that she whelps one should be able to know which is the right period for mating. Cavaliers as a breed are very prone to whelp two to three days early and if they go beyond their time there is nearly always something wrong. If they don't whelp to the day they should immediately be taken to the veterinary surgeon. This may sound strange to breeders of other breeds, but in twenty years of breeding the author has only had one bitch whelp late and everything's been all right. On the other occasions when bitches have gone over time there has been something wrong.

Provided the mating has been satisfactory there is no need at all for a repetition, it is only really of use when a bitch is difficult to get into whelp. Some experts even go so far as to say that provided the first mating has taken, a second one may upset it.

Cavaliers should present no difficulties over matings; they are natural little dogs and on the whole like to do the whole thing themselves without a great deal of interference, but a little help is sometimes necessary.

The Bitch in Whelp

There may be little sign that a Cavalier bitch is in whelp until after the fourth week. It may be that she may seem a little quiet or a bit off colour during the early weeks, but more often than not there is no sign. By the fifth week there should be a slight thickening of the flanks, and the nipples will become slightly enlarged. It is always advisable to worm the bitch after she has been mated. Three weeks after mating is a good time, but there are some veterinary surgeons and breeders who advise worming again later on. The most sensible thing for the novice is to enlist the veterinary surgeon's help and he will prescribe for the individual dog.

Food at that period should be normal, but as the pregnancy advances more proteins and less starch should be used. Three Canoval tablets a day should be given and also calcium tablets which can be obtained from the vet. It is most important to give these two items.

The in-whelp bitch should not be allowed to become fat with flabby tissue as this will not make for an easy whelping. In fact if she is too fat at the time of mating it may stop her conceiving. She should have plenty of exercise and not be treated as an invalid, but towards the end of her pregnancy she should be allowed to take her exercise at her own pace and other dogs should not be allowed to worry her or play roughly with her. If she is to whelp in a certain box in a certain room she must have time to accustom herself to this before whelping.

The bitch who is the complete pet of the whole house should be allowed to stay in the house. If she is suddenly put outside she may be very miserable and even leave her puppies to get back to the house. A warm kitchen is an ideal place for this, and if wanted it may be quite an easy thing to transfer the mother and her babies outside in about a week or ten days' time. Most breeders will have heated whelping quarters with the addition of the infra-ray lamp mentioned in the previous chapter.

The first sign that will be seen of fairly imminent whelping is the making of a nest. Her box should be filled with newspaper and this she can tear up to her heart's content. She should be carefully watched from about four to five days before the date due for whelping. Some bitches have a passion to make their nest under a garden shed and it can be extremely difficult to get them out from underneath.

Heat is an essential factor during the first few days after birth and the ideal temperature should be around 75° Fahrenheit. The temperature should remain at this level for the first three or four days, and this enables the puppies to utilize all their food for growing purposes. If they are cold a larger proportion of this food will have to go towards making their central heating and they will not thrive as well as puppies kept in a warm temperature or under a lamp.

Healthy puppies are quiet and contented-looking. Mewling puppies are unhealthy ones and there may be a variety of reasons for this. The bitch's milk could be sour, they may not be sucking properly or there may be some infection which will cause fading puppies.

The Whelping Box. This should be an open-topped box with three sides solid and the front divided into two parts, thus enabling the bitch to get out and the puppies kept in or vice versa.

It is a good idea to have a rail about three and a half inches from the floor around the inside of the box. This will help to prevent the bitch squashing a puppy by getting it into a corner and lying on it. As a rule Cavaliers are gentle mothers, but they can be a bit clumsy about turning round.

Newspaper is really the easiest thing to whelp on; it can be replaced easily during the process and is more easy to dispose of than old blankets or rugs. It is also exceedingly good to keep the puppies and mother on in the early stages and is easier too for the mother to keep clean. When they get bigger, after four to five weeks, a soft wood wool such as Abbotts Sanibed is excellent. It is clean and hygienic and has a pleasant woody smell. This can be used at an earlier age, particularly in cold weather when the family make more use of a nest, but newspaper is quite adequate in the early stages and far less expensive.

Whelping. Cavaliers, particularly maiden bitches, like to have someone they know with them during whelping, but the person must not be oversensitive and fussy. Cavaliers are very prone to assimilate any moods or feelings that their owners have. and a slightly nervous bitch will be made far worse by a rather hysterical owner, whereas a very calm person can help enormously to make the whelping easier. Unless you are taken entirely by surprise it is always advisable to supervise the whelping, even if not there all the time. By so doing puppies may often be saved who would otherwise have died.

There are various signs of imminent whelping which may or may not take place.

1. The making of the nest and tearing up of newspaper.
2. Obvious restlessness and slight discomfort.
3. Panting. This may come later, but Cavaliers are very prone to pant from the first signs onwards.
4. A drop in temperature from the normal 101.4°F (38.5°C).
5. Lack of appetite; although this is not a sure sign, as some bitches can wolf an enormous meal and an hour later have their puppies.
6. The commencement of straining; these pains are the passing of the puppy down the passage culminating in the more severe uterine contractions needed to expel the puppy.

These pains are quite visible and may go on for some hours before a puppy is born, and in fact a slow birth is better for the bitch than a very quick one.

The first thing to be seen is a rather black-looking bag of membranes at the exit to the vulva. This will appear and disappear with the contractions, each time emerging a little more. This bag is filled with fluid with the puppy inside, and the fluid is to protect the puppy during its voyage down the birth passage.

When the bag is almost out, if it seems to have got rather stuck it may be manually eased out with the rhythm of the contractions. For this purpose either a pair of sterilized rubber gloves or sterilized lint is needed, as the sac is very slippery. It should come out perfectly easily on its own with the puppy's head inside – head first. Sometimes we get what is called a 'breech birth', which is the rump coming first; provided the puppy is still in its sac this should present no problems.

Should the water sac burst, and no puppy appear, after an hour the veterinary surgeon should be called. A dry birth is not good for either mother or puppy and a dry breech birth will nearly always need assistance.

After the puppy has appeared, complete with placenta, the mother will break the sac, thus enabling the puppy's head to come out and for it to breathe. She will eat the placenta and bite the umbilical cord to within a short distance of the navel. Should she fail to do this it must be done for her. The sac must be broken as quickly as possible, the umbilical cord cut with sterilized scissors and iodine put on the end of the cord. The placenta is then thrown in the fire or wrapped in paper and thrown away afterwards. If the puppy is left in the sac it will die of asphyxiation.

The next step is for the bitch to lick the puppy dry. This she will do in quite a rough manner and it is done with a purpose. It is to stimulate the circulation and establish a separate circulation from that of the mother. If she doesn't do this the puppy should be rubbed in a dry warm Turkish towel until full movement has been promoted and it is yelling lustily. It should then be given back to the mother.

Some breeders advocate taking the puppies away after birth and putting them in a warm basket with a hot-water bottle under the towels until whelping has finished. My own view is that provided the puppies are watched to see they don't get too cold, or too wet with the subsequent sacs breaking, it is better to leave them with the mother, who may get very distressed without them. Also some of them suck almost as soon as they are born and this has a stimulating action on the uterus.

The intervals between the births vary, they can come every quarter of an hour or there can be an hour's interval between them. Provided the bitch is resting quietly during the intervals there is no need to worry, as this is a natural performance. During a long birth a drink of luke-warm milk and glucose is much appreciated by the bitch.

When the breeder can feel no more puppies in the womb, and the last puppy is quite dry, the bitch should be taken outside for a few moments to relieve herself. The soiled bedding should be replaced with clean and she can then settle down with her family for a good sleep.

Feeding of the Bitch. For forty-eight hours after whelping a light diet only should be given consisting of milky food, eggs, fish and perhaps a little tripe. She may want to be fed by hand, and in any case will always want to be fed in with her babies. The stomach after whelping is in a slightly delicate condition and red meat and a lot of starch will overload it. If she has eaten the placentas she will pass black motions, possibly with a little blood in them, but this is merely the turning out of what she has eaten. Should she have diarrhoea for several days, some form of medicine should be given. It is really best to obtain this from the veterinary surgeon and may be in liquid form or in crystals.

The bitch will probably be most reluctant to leave her puppies even for a short while, but short periods of time outside, with a little walking about, are essential to keep the bowels working and also the bladder emptied. As soon as she has performed this task she can go straight back to her puppies.

The quiet nursery is very important at this time and the puppies should not be handled more than necessary. Most Cavaliers are extremely good-tempered with all and sundry, but even they do not like their offspring picked up by strangers. They should also be kept in a quiet place and children should not be allowed to bother them.

The normal-size litter for a Cavalier is four to five, but they have been known to have eleven. This is far too many for them and either a foster-mother should be found or some put down. It is of course possible to hand-rear puppies, but they should be allowed to have the bitch's colostrum, which is the first milk, and she should also clean them. The licking stimulates the inside of the puppies and makes the insides work.

It is essential to feed the bitch very well – at least four meals a day should be given. Breakfast should consist of some milky substance such as Farlene, Benger's Food or Laughing Dog Milk food, etc., with glucose added and possibly a raw egg whipped up in it. Tinned rice pudding is also good. Luncheon should be the best meat or fish with a little soaked meal. Dinner the same and supper the same as breakfast, and she should be given as much milk and water as necessary. Also as well she should have calcium tablets to prevent eclampsia. Cavaliers are very generous mothers and are prone to this affliction. It is a calcium deficiency and oddly enough the better condition the bitch is in the more likely she is to go down with it. Should this happen the veterinary surgeon should be called at once and will give calcium intravenously. Failure to do this will probably cause the death of the bitch. The signs are excessive panting, staggering on the legs, or complete collapse. This is by no means a thing that happens at every whelping, but owing to the fact that Cavaliers are prone to it, it should be watched for. It can also happen before whelping, but this is much more rare.

These four meals should be continued the whole time the bitch is feeding the puppies, but the intake of liquid should be decreased gradually from the fifth week onwards, so that the milk will not be encouraged and will begin to dry up. The puppies should be fully weaned from the dam at six and a half weeks, or at the latest seven weeks.

Weaning. The sooner the puppies begin to lap, the better, for this will augment the bitch's milk and take some of the strain off her. One of the easiest ways is to put a large flat sandwich tin with milk food in it so that the puppies may lap with the mother. This should be started from three weeks old, or just after. As soon as they get used to lapping they will want some more substantial food, such as meat. Ideally this should be raw scraped beef, but other kinds of meat can be fed. Cooked meat, minced very finely, or even one of the frozen packs may be used, but there is no doubt that fresh meat is by far the best and has most nutriment in it. A little very fine puppy meal may be added to this – Spiller's Puppy Savil No. 1 is excellent. All meal should be soaked until all the liquid has been absorbed. It should never be fed sloppy. The amount of food should gradually be increased until the puppies are on their full four meals a day – two milk food meals and two meat meals. By this time the bitch's milk will have started to dry up, and although she will still sleep with her family, and they will still try to suck her, they won't get much nourishment and should be taken completely away from her at least by seven weeks old.

Some form of bonemeal and halibut-liver oil should also be given at this age, a teaspoonful in food. Calicol D is now obtainable again. If the puppies are sufficiently advanced they will be able to eat their Canoval tablets but if not, one of the proprietary brands of bonemeal should be added with a couple of drops of halibut-liver oil per puppy to one meal of the day.

It is a very good thing to give the puppies something to chew on to help their second teeth to come in. It can be some form of biscuit or it can be a marrow bone. The puppies will eat about a large saucer full of food at this age and this must, of course, be gradually increased with the growth of the puppy.

Goats' milk is very good, as we said in the chapter on General Management, but if cows' milk is given care should be taken to water down the Channel Island breeds' milk. This contains too rich a butter-fat content and will upset the tender insides of the young Cavalier. Lactol is excellent to start the young puppies off.

To enlarge on why the Channel Island breeds' milk must be watered down, a look at the following chart may be of some use.

	Butter Fat %	Protein %	Lactos %	Mineral %	Total Solids %
Goat	4.09	3.71	4.20	0.78	14.00
Jersey	5.14		9.43		15.57
Friesian	3.14		8.48		12.30
Ayrshire	3.85		8.87		12.72

As a rule the size of the fat globules increases with the percentage of butter fat and this is the difficult thing for a young puppy to digest. It will be seen, therefore, that the Jersey has almost 2 per cent more total solids and 1 per cent higher butter fat than goats' milk. The breakdown of the Guernsey milk is similar to the Jersey with a high butter-fat content. Some veterinary surgeons go so far as to say that they never give Channel Island milk to young puppies as no amount of added water will reduce the size of the fat globules or total solid content. If the milk is watered down, the young stomach will obviously not have so many fat globules to deal with and, while certainly not being an ideal food, is certainly better than the plain Channel Island milk if nothing else is available.

We will leave the feeding of the seven-week-old puppy and return to other things that should take place in its early life.

Docking of Tails and Dew Claws
The docking of tails is optional, but if it is to be done it should

be done together with the dew claws on the fourth or fifth day. If the puppies are very large at birth, it may be done on the third day. For the novice it is advisable to ask the veterinary surgeon to do this. It is not a difficult operation but needs a certain amount of practice.

The utensils needed are two pairs of scissors, one of the pairs having a ribbed effect at the end, and the other being moderately pointed and sharp. The third utensil is a special pair of scissors with a hole in the middle especially for docking tails. All these utensils must be sterilized. If the tail is to be docked, one-third is removed. The method is quite simple. Get someone to hold the puppy, measure off one-third of the tail, put the special scissors round the tail and gently squeeze until it is cut through. Hold the scissors in this position for a minute to clamp the ends of the veins and then remove. Anoint gently with a styptic pencil or permanganate of potash and all should be well. It is advisable to do all this in surgical rubber gloves, for if the styptic pencil gets on to the hands it will leave a stain that only comes out with time. Now for the dew claws – this is slightly more tricky, as everything is so small.

Cavaliers seldom have hind dew claws, but it can happen – therefore, the hind legs must be checked. Should they be there, the procedure for removal is the same. Hold the paw firmly in the left hand, take the ridged pair of scissors and get the point underneath the dew claw. It will then pop out and the scissors should be squeezed as hard as possible to stop bleeding. After a minute remove those scissors and with the other pair snip off the dew claw which is now protruding. Repeat on the other leg. Anoint with the styptic pencil or permanganate of potash and return to the nest. Should bleeding occur on either the tail or dew claws, cover the wound with a piece of cotton wool and hold hard above the wound. This acts like a tourniquet and should stop any bleeding. The puppies must be checked for a while afterwards to make sure that all bleeding has stopped. They will nearly always squeal during this operation, but at that early age it is doubtful if much pain is felt.

Should a delay take place and the tail and dew claws are not done at that early age they should be left until quite a bit later on and then done by the veterinary surgeon under an anaesthetic.

The reason for removing the dew claws is not only for beauty's sake, for they can catch in brambles, get torn and become very painful.

Some bitches become very upset at hearing their puppies squealing, in which case they are best removed; others take it all in their stride and comfort the poor sufferers as soon as they are put back in the nest.

The wounds will heal very quickly and no ill-effects should be noticed at all. Cavalier puppies are not very advanced babies. Unlike some breeds they like to take life leisurely. The eyes will open at about ten days and they may then start to wander in the box a little, but very often the highly contented litter will just remain like little puddings, very often head to tail, until about two and a half weeks. During this time, and after, the puppies' nails will grow and become very sharp. This is not only painful for the mother but will cause abrasions on her tummy and can also cause sores on the other puppies. Although the puppies should be allowed to wander on a hard surface, the nails must be kept trimmed. Just trim off the end curved bit of the nail in the same way as the older dogs were dealt with.

If possible the box for mother and puppies should be in a nice light place where sunlight, if any, can penetrate. Not too much sun, of course, but this happens only rarely in England. The mother will clean up all the messes in the first three weeks, but care should be taken that the newspaper is changed constantly so that the bed is always fresh.

When the puppies begin to move about it is a very good idea to have a small run attached to the whelping box. Puppies don't like fouling their own bed and will most likely go outside to relieve themselves. This run should also be kept covered with newspaper and constantly changed.

If the weather is really warm there is no reason why mother and babies at this age cannot be put out into the garden. A shady place should be chosen, well out of draughts, with possibly a patch at the end of the run where the sun strikes.

The puppies should still not be handled by many people for fear of infection.

Worming

Cavalier puppies suffer badly from worms, irrespective of the bitch having been wormed, and they should be treated between four and five weeks old.

The signs of worms, apart from seeing them in the motions, are a staring coat, a pot belly, and a generally non-thriving puppy.

Every litter should be done, but some have to be done before others. It is round worms which infest the poor mites at this age and the only satisfactory method of worming is to obtain some tablets from the veterinary surgeon. Either a whole, half or quarter tablet is given according to weight, but full directions will be given by the veterinary surgeon. These tablets are quite easy to give. Just open the puppy's mouth, place the pill on the back of the tongue, give it a tiny push, shut the puppy's mouth and massage the throat gently. Care must be taken that the tablet is not retained in the mouth and then spat out.

On the day of the worming the bitch should be kept away from the puppies all day. If she is not kept away she will clean up all the worms and then reinfest herself. This is important. The dosing should be repeated in two weeks' time.

The next important occasion in the puppy's life is inoculation.

The ordinary injection against hard pad, distemper and hepatitis is not now done until eleven and a half or twelve weeks old. It used to be done at nine weeks, but there have been several breakdowns and the makers (and there are more than one) of these inoculations advise the later date for injecting. There is a preparation called Gamatative which can be given at an early age if hard pad and distemper are known to be in the vicinity; it will give an immunity for two to three weeks.

There is, however, an inoculation which is in two parts. The first can be done at eight weeks and the second three weeks later. This also combines the leptospirosis inoculation. The immunity will not become effective until a week after the first inoculation, and prospective buyers should be warned of this.

There is a constant research going on into immunization of dogs from these canine diseases, and it is always advisable to ask the veterinary surgeon what boosters he advises and when.

At the risk of repetition it cannot be emphasized too strongly that the well-being of the puppy very largely depends on feeding in early life. Adequate facilities for play, warmth and cleanliness are also very necessary.

Parasites

Puppies can be beset with lice and these are generally found around the ears and up the legs, especially in very dry weather.

A well-looked-after kennel should not have this problem, but it can easily crop up and should be watched for. If these little horrors are found they must be got rid of at once, and advice should be sought from a qualified person. Some of the louse powders on the open market are too strong for the young puppy and an alternative must be found. In the case of lice being present, the bitch must also be treated, as it is almost certain that she will have the parasites too.

Fleas during the summer months, and particularly where the bitch goes into long grass, may be very prevalent. Here again care must be taken not to put too strong a powder on to the bitch which may affect the puppies' noses while sucking.

It is a good idea to check the bitch thoroughly about a week before she is due to whelp. If any fleas are found she can be sprayed with Nuvan Top and well brushed and combed through before the arrival of the puppies. It is also most necessary to clean the ears of the bitch for some weeks before whelping with a good ear dressing against ear mites. These are tiny creatures that live in the ear and can't be seen by the human eye. They are generally passed on by cats. They cause great irritation and subsequent scratching, which may then result in eczema in the ear and even an abscess. She will pass these mites on to her puppies and then they will start scratching, with the subsequent results. It is advisable to obtain this dressing from the veterinary surgeon.

The other thing that it is advisable to do about a week before whelping is to cut the feathers on her b ittom. This will enable her to keep herself clean and also preclude any risk of the puppies getting tied up in long feathers; she will lose all her coat, in any case, after whelping, so no harm will be done.

False Pregnancy

This is not uncommon and the bitch will even go so far as to produce milk.

This condition is caused by a stimulation of the reproductive hormones due to the act of mating.

Should there be an orphaned litter of puppies a Cavalier can and will take these on under these conditions and rear them.

Usually the milk will dry up naturally and the bitch return to normal. Unless absolutely necessary, it is very unwise either to try to draw off the milk or to massage the breasts. This will merely stimulate the milk glands and produce more.

Another, so-called, false pregnancy is when the bitch actually is definitely in whelp at four weeks and then has no puppies. In this case the embryonic puppies are dissolved and absorbed by the tissues of the bitch. This could be caused by a toxic condition, or even a premature fall causing the death of the embryo. It could also be caused by a lethal hereditary factor.

In any case, if a bitch has missed more than once, it is wise to ask the advice of the veterinary surgeon.

There are injections that can be given. Firstly at the time of mating to stimulate conception, and secondly at three to four weeks after mating to help the bitch hold on to the puppies.

8

Sickness in Cavaliers

THIS chapter is in no way a veterinary guide, but with every breed of dog there are various ailments to which they are more prone than others, and which can be watched for. Veterinary advice can then be sought more quickly with this slight knowledge. There are several natural hazards which can easily be avoided or circumvented.

Cavaliers are a hardy, sporting breed. They should not be mollycoddled and love hunting and are good water dogs. They have the good hunting nose of an ordinary spaniel and can make very good retrievers for the smaller type of bird.

We have already spoken about the necessity for inoculation against hard pad, distemper, canine virus hepatitis and leptospirosis. This is a 'must' and is the first step in protection against illness. A constant careful observation of any dog will show if there are any signs of it being 'off colour'. Should this occur the temperature should be taken, and provided there is no great rise (in which case veterinary advice *must* be sought at once) the dog should be kept warm, put on a light diet and watched for further developments. Should sickness and diarrhoea begin this could be the beginning of gastroenteritis and the veterinary surgeon should be contacted if it continues for more than twenty-four hours or if blood is present.

Always starve a vomiting animal and give water in frequent but very small quantities only. Don't give any meat and milk while the diarrhoea is present; give the dog only water and dry biscuits such as arrowroot or plain sponge cakes.

There are many excellent preparations in liquid, tablet or granule form for this complaint, which can be obtained from the veterinary surgeon and are always useful to keep in the house or kennel in case of emergencies.

Both forms of leptospirosis are often difficult to diagnose in the early stages. The *leptospira icterohaemorrhagiae* is a rapid and very often fatal jaundice carried by rats and passed on by their urine. It can also be transmitted to humans. The liver and kidneys are attacked and badly damaged, often before any sign is seen. A constant vomiting and excessive drinking are two of the symptoms. Inoculation should prevent this, but a booster should be given every year.

The other leptospira is canicola, which can be transmitted to humans by the urine of an infected dog. It is quite possible for a dog to contract this disease in a very mild form, so that it may not even be recognized, but could easily be the cause of nephritis in an older dog. Although it can be immediately fatal, it is more likely to be the cause of death in later years.

When a temperature is taken an ordinary clinical thermometer with a blunt nose should be used; long-nosed thermometers are inadvisable for fear of breaking off the long tip which contains the mercury. The thermometer should be gently inserted into the rectum for about an inch and then left in that position for about a minute. It should be held the whole time while it is in the rectum and should the dog object violently to this, it must be held by another person. Most Cavaliers make no fuss over this, but it is wise to be on the look-out for resistance.

Many of our human diseases are also suffered by dogs. Pneumonia, both the virus and other form, are quite common. Diabetes is also known, but is not a very common complaint. Daily insulin injections can be given as in humans, but with a much older dog it really is kinder to put it down. Heart trouble is very often caused by overweight and that, in its turn, can be caused by thyroid trouble.

If a Cavalier is on an entirely starch-free diet and still continues to put on excessive weight it may well be due to thyroid trouble. This can be diagnosed by a veterinary surgeon and pills can be given to counteract this. An over- or under-active thyroid will also cause lethargy and can make an otherwise clean house dog into a dirty one.

Should a perfectly house-trained Cavalier suddenly become very dirty there is usually a reason for it other than just naughtiness, and veterinary advice should be taken.

Certainly in the older dog there may be many reasons for becoming dirty. Excessive urinating may be the onset of an uraemic condition or a failing of the kidneys. Under these circumstances it is the natural cessation, through old age, of the functional organs, and the veterinary surgeon may well advise the putting-down of the poor sufferer. A very strong urine smell will come from the dog's mouth. If any blood is seen in the urine this could be caused by kidney or bladder stones, but this is not a common complaint in Cavaliers.

Again it cannot be emphasized too strongly that at the first indication of any of these symptoms veterinary advice should be sought at once.

To return to the human ailments. Pneumonia has a peculiar kind of rasping breathing. The temperature will also rise rapidly and antibiotics must be given at once. These will generally bring the temperature down rapidly, but this by no means is the end of the illness. Great care and nursing for some time afterwards is essential. The dog must be kept very warm and quiet, and if it *must* go out to relieve itself a warm knitted coat should be put on while it is out. In the early stages it is warm and comforting to have the knitted coat on all the time, like humans used to wear a pneumonia jacket. The temperature must be constantly watched and any rapid change should be reported immediately to the veterinary surgeon.

Heart conditions are very often prefaced by constant panting and extreme lethargy. The dog may even have fainting fits.

Some heart conditions are characterized by a persistent choking cough, therefore again expert advice should be sought if this condition continues.

Cancer can also occur in dogs and this, as in humans, is more often than not undetectable in the very early stages. Having eventually been diagnosed, the veterinary surgeon's advice as to whether or not an operation is necessary, must be taken.

Eclampsia we have already spoken of, so there is no need to go into further details here.

Eczema. This is a non-contagious inflammatory condition of the skin generally accompanied by itching. It may be either moist or dry. Eczema has many causes – improper diet, external or internal parasites, allergy, hormone deficiency, or simply a lack of hygiene. It is essential to eliminate the cause as well as to treat the condition. Most cases respond rapidly to treatment with a cortisone derivative. This can be administered either as an injection, tablets by mouth, or as an ointment or lotion. In bad cases a combination of the three may be used, but it must be done under veterinary supervision. Benzyl Benzoate lotion is an easily obtained and inexpensive remedy which is frequently beneficial in cases of dry eczema, but should not be used if the skin is broken.

Mange is one of the most unpleasant of the skin diseases. There are two kinds and one of them is contagious to humans and animals. This is sarcoptic mange, more commonly known as scabies. It is caused by a burrowing parasite and will give intense irritation and subsequent scratching. The lesions usually appear on the abdomen, chest and legs, and also in the edges of the ear flaps, which then become thickened and very irritating. Sarcoptic mange is exceedingly contagious, so prompt diagnosis followed by thorough treatment and hygiene is essential.

The other kind of mange is demodectic or follicular mange. This is caused by a parasite which actually lives in the follicles (roots) of the hair. It is not contagious but is frequently hereditary. Luckily it is a relatively uncommon complaint in Cavaliers. Lesions appear as bare thickened areas of skin usually under the elbows and on the limbs. These areas frequently show black or grey pigmentation and have a distinctive 'mousy' odour. Dogs with this form of mange do not show the intense irritation of those suffering from sarcoptic mange, but it is very much more difficult to cure, so prompt diagnosis is of great importance.

With careful grooming, that should be done at least two or three times a week, any sign of these two manges should be apparent in the early stages and the veterinary surgeon visited at once.

The long-coated dog, which a Cavalier is, can be afflicted by some of these eczemas through not being constantly groomed. A lot of dead hair in a profuse coat will cause an irritation and consequent eczema, so it is not only for beauty's sake that constant grooming is essential.

Ringworm is another form of skin disease. This is highly contagious both to humans and dogs and generally, again, is present in young animals or children. It is quite easily seen as it does exactly what its name says. The fungus causes small round practically bare patches on the skin. It is very often seen on the face and can appear on other parts of the body.

Every skin complaint should be taken to the veterinary surgeon for analysis. They are often very difficult for the layman to differentiate, and if wrong treatment is given, will naturally prolong the illness.

I think that the snake bite, although not a contagious illness, should certainly be mentioned in this chapter.

There are a great many adders in the South of England and these are the only snakes with a dangerous bite. These need not be fatal, but prompt action should be taken. Most bites around the face are less dangerous than around the legs. On the feet is the most dangerous. A tourniquet should be applied for not longer than half an hour without temporary relaxation and the dog taken to the veterinary surgeon as soon as possible. If the bite is visible and can be cut, the poison should then be sucked out. At all times keep the dog warm, give it a little brandy if available, or tea or coffee with plenty of sugar. Treatment by injection with anti-venom is advisable, as although most cases would recover naturally, they are liable to be left with a damaged heart.

Wasp and bee stings. These are very common and although not usually dangerous, unless the sting is internal, they can cause great distress. The simplest remedy for a wasp sting is vinegar, which can be applied direct to the sting, or administered by mouth if the wasp has been swallowed and has stung the dog internally. Bee stings are acid, so must be treated differently from wasp stings. Either ammonia, bicarbonate of soda, or blue bag are effective.

Worms. There are three kinds of common worms – the round, the tape, and the hook. The round worms can be seen easily in the motions of an infected dog and look like spaghetti. In some cases these can be vomited up. The tape will also be seen in the motions and are small flat white segments of the worm itself. These segments may also be seen on the hairs around the anus of the dog. The hookworm is a very unpleasant creature, but luckily is not very common in this country, but it can occur and can be serious, as it will cause haemorrhage in the intestines and anaemia. There is not much outward sign of it, but a laboratory test of the motions will confirm whether or not this particular worm is present.

With all these three pests the only safe and reliable way to deal with them is by remedies given by the veterinary surgeon. The other remedies sold over the counter are not nearly as effective.

Coccidiosis. This is another type of internal parasite which causes chronic dysentery and debility. It is not very prevalent, but should be considered in all unexplained cases of persistent diarrhoea. Both hookworm and coccidiosis can be the cause of hysteria and convulsions. Rabbits and fleas are great tapeworm carriers.

If the coat has no shine on it and looks rather 'starey', this is probably an indication that some kind of worm is present. Dogs can very easily re-infect themselves, and as worming is not the drastic operation that it used to be, it is not a bad idea to give them a worming about once a year. Of course, if the worms are seen, it must be done at once.

One of the natural hazards about which one can do nothing is the poisons that are now to be found in agriculture. Much has been written on this subject with regard to birds, and the mortality has been very high with these poor little creatures.

Infected meat will produce a grave toxic poisoning in the animal that has eaten it. It will produce excessive vomiting and diarrhoea and can easily kill.

Although by law poison is not allowed to be laid on the ground in a trap, this unfortunately is sometimes done, and the Cavalier, who we know is a very sporting and hunting dog, can pick up some bait and will die in great pain.

Many weedkillers are also poisonous to dogs, and also rat killers. Great care should always be taken never to let a dog run loose where there is any chance of any poison.

Slug poison is extremely dangerous to dogs and can cause death in convulsions within a very short time if not treated immediately. Unfortunately slug bait pellets seem to have a fatal fascination for dogs, so great care should be exercised if there is any reason to believe that they have been put down anywhere.

In all cases where a dog is suspected of having recently swallowed poison it is a wise precaution to make the animal vomit. This can quite easily be done by pushing a few small lumps of washing soda down its throat.

Ticks are very easily picked up and are just as easily removed. A pair of tweezers which will get right underneath the head of the tick is a good instrument to use. Make sure that the head is right out. You will see tentacles coming from the head which will be moving if the whole thing has been removed. A few drops of turpentine placed on the tick will cause it to drop off and this may be the easier method for a novice. Ticks are very easily seen, for having gorged on the blood of the animal, they will become fairly large and grey. There is now a tick spray on the market which will make the ticks drop off.

The normal span of life for a healthy Cavalier is eleven or twelve years. Provided there is nothing organically wrong they will begin to fade like any human who reaches a great age. Blindness, deafness, and general lassitude may set in, also they tend to become very smelly. When this condition becomes apparent, and obviously life is not being enjoyed, the kindest thing to do is to ask the veterinary surgeon to put the dog down. This is done so painlessly that they won't even know it is being done and will go into a deep sleep from which they never wake up. If it can be done in their own environment it is a much happier way to do it.

After all, they have been good and constant companions for a long time and it is a small thing to do on our part to make their end as happy as possible.

9

The Show Ring

SHOWING a Cavalier is not only a pleasant and enjoyable pastime but it is also quite an art. The showing of any animal is an art and some people have it, some acquire it and some will never have it. A great many people have what is termed 'an eye' for an animal and whether it is dogs, horses or cows they can often pick out the best while knowing relatively nothing about the breed. This is because they have a natural instinct for a balanced animal. Nothing can be really good unless its conformation is correct, neither can it be balanced.

Of course, there is no such thing as a perfect animal, or human for that matter, but minor faults can often be hidden by a clever showman.

If the intending exhibitor really thinks he has been bitten by the bug he will be very wise, both for his own sake and for that of the young hopeful, to enter in the breed classes at the smaller shows, so that both can learn the ways and means before entering the higher stakes. After all, everyone must learn his job and the puppy who is pitchforked straight away into a large noisy environment with a novice owner may never want to do it again. Some Cavaliers are natural showers, but many are not, and they can stand with every part of them in the wrong position, thereby making a perfectly sound dog look appalling.

Cavalier owners and breeders are a happy and generous band of people and are only too happy to help the novice till they can stand on their own feet. By going to several of the smaller shows where breed judges are scheduled it should be possible to ascertain whether or not your particular dog has show potentialities.

The difference between a breed judge and an all-rounder is that the former does what the name implies – judges the breed exclusively, whereas the all-rounder judges many, if not all, breeds. From the breed point of view it is a good thing, certainly for the Championship Shows, to have a good balance between these two types, but I think it is probably more instructive for the novice exhibitor to show under breed judges at the smaller shows to start off with.

All the shows are advertised in either *Our Dogs* or *Dog World*, mostly with the names of the judges. The secretary of the chosen show should be written to and asked to send a schedule. Entries for the smaller shows generally close a couple of weeks prior to the show, and for the Championship Shows they close a month before. Entries vary from about £1 a class at Sanction Shows to well over £4 for the first class at Championship Shows.

There are four kinds of shows licensed and approved by the Kennel Club. Whichever type of show it is is stated in the advertisement and K.C. rules and regulations are printed inside every schedule. The biggest is the Championship Show; this can be for a variety of breeds or can be held by the Breed Club. Application has to be made to the Kennel Club every year for championship status. The Kennel Club having granted this status then offers a set of Challenge Certificates, one for dogs and one for bitches. To become a champion, three of these Certificates must be won by a dog under three different judges. The number of sets of Certificates given to the different breeds depends on the number of their registrations, and because a breed is scheduled at a Championship Show it does not necessarily mean that they will have Certificates on offer there.

The next show in order of importance is the Open Show. This is virtually the same as the Championship Show, except there are no Challenge Certificates. This kind of show can again be held by a Society or a Breed Club and like the Championship Show is open to anyone. At some Championship Shows no prize money is offered and at Cruft's, the 'show of all shows', you have to qualify your dog for entry – the qualifications vary from year to year.

A Limited Show is confined to members of the Society or the Breed Club, as is a Sanction Show. The latter is also restricted as to the number of its classes, twenty for a variety show and ten for a breed show. No dog who has won a Challenge Certificate is eligible for this type of show and the classes do not go higher than Post-Graduate.

There is one other kind of show which is held by permission of the Kennel Club and is called an Exemption Show. This is generally held in aid of a charity and attracts a great many entries. There have to be four pedigree classes such as A.V. Puppy or A.V. Non-Sporting or A.V. Toy or something like that, and then a number of novelty classes such as 'the dog who wags its tail the longest', 'the dog with the most soulful eyes', etc. For this kind of show, in the latter classes, the dogs need not be registered at the Kennel Club.

There is an honour which only a young dog of up to eighteen months can win and this is the Junior Warrant. This was instituted by the Kennel Club just prior to 1939 and can be claimed for a dog which wins twenty-five points before the age of eighteen months. These points are awarded as follows:

Three points for a first prize at a Championship Show in breed classes open to all and where Challenge Certificates are offered.

One point for a first prize at an Open Show in a breed class open to all exhibitors.

There are various schools of thought about the advisability of trying to gain this award. A really good specimen of the breed should have little trouble in gaining his Junior Warrant, but it is most inadvisable to overshow a young dog just for the chance of doing this. Over-showing will undoubtedly defeat its own ends and will result in ring-staleness and general boredom which may wreck his hopes of future high honours.

Once an exhibit is out of puppy it will then have to compete against much stiffer opposition from older dogs. He will probably by that time be ineligible for novice classes and will therefore have to go into the higher class with consequently less chance of winning a first at a Championship Show. This may result in touring the Open Shows with the consequent results that have been mentioned. A Junior Warrant is a very nice award to have and one to be proud of, but care must be taken not to sicken the dog of the ring.

The Kennel Club is the ruling body in dogdom and every win and award has to be checked by them, and, in the case of Challenge Certificates and Junior Warrants, confirmed by them. If a dog is entered in a class for which he is ineligible, and wins a prize, this will be found out on checking and the dog will be disqualified. Therefore, it is most essential to keep a correct record of all wins, which enables the owner at a glance to see for what he is eligible.

No dog is allowed to be shown at any show (other than those certain classes at any Exemption) unless it is registered at the Kennel Club and transferred into the new owner's name, therefore the first thing to do is to make sure that your dog is registered and transferred from the breeder's name into your name.

The whole system of registration has recently been changed. Therefore, after applying to the Kennel Club for the appropriate form, it is advisable to read it carefully and to check with the K.C. on any points you don't understand.

To put it as simply as possible, there are three stages of the registration system.

1. The recording of the litter. This is essential for further registering, as you will see in the following stages, and should be done before the litter is three months old, after which the fee is much more.
2. The registration of individual dogs on to the Basic Register.
3. Active Register. This is essential if they are to be bred from, shown, entered for Obedience or Field Trials, or exported.

These three stages may all be done at the same time on the one form or, once the litter is recorded, at a later date. Should you be the proud possessor of a registered affix you must use it before the dog leaves your ownership. When you sell a puppy or older dog it must then be transferred into the new owner's name together with the K.C. papers, a transfer form, a copy of the pedigree signed by the breeder and the Certificate of Inoculation if this has been done. Providing it is already on the Active Register the new owner can show it at once even if the transfer has not come through by putting T.A.F. on the entry form. If a new owner wishes to add his affix to the dog's name, this can be done by putting his kennel name as a suffix, i.e. after the dog's name, provided his dog is on the Active Register. This cannot be done once a dog has been entered in the Stud Book. Any dog winning a first, second or third in the Open Class (open to all Colours) at a Championship Show will automatically gain entry into the Stud Book.

This will most likely only happen to a dog older than six months and the owner will have been notified of the Stud Book number allocated to the dog and be able to pass it on to the new owner.

This change of name is hardly likely to apply to the novice as it is improbable at this early stage that a prefix or affix will have been registered. The object of having a prefix or affix is to enable people to recognize a dog from a certain kennel.

Before entering a dog for a show a certain amount of ring training should be given. It is to be hoped that the lead and walking training as described in Chapter 6 will have been done.

Certain restrictions have been put into practice at some of the Championship Shows, whereby a dog has to qualify to gain the right to enter the show. Cruft's is one of these shows where there are qualifications, but these are always open to revision and will change from time to time. Any restrictions are always clearly marked in the schedule.

Show Preparation
All things being equal, we have now arrived at the important moment of the 'first' show.

Blenheims and Tricolours should be bathed in a good shampoo the day before the show. Sometimes if the coat tends to be a little curly or 'fly-away' it is advisable to put an old silk or nylon stocking on the dog and leave it on until it is time to go to the show. No trimming of any kind is necessary for show. Cavaliers are supposed to be a natural breed and their feathering is part of their charm.

Black/Tans and Rubies need not be bathed. If they are it should be done several days beforehand to give time for the sheen to come back on their coats. This is where the chamois

leather or silk handkerchief comes into use. Another good
thing to rub the back with is a velvet glove.

We are fortunate in our breed that we do not have to use
chalk. The white on the Blenheims and Tricolours should be a
pearly white and not a dead white.

The next thing is the preparation of the show bag. This
should contain:

1. A warm blanket to put in the pen for the dog to sit on.
2. A towel in case any cleaning up is necessary.
3. A spirit shampoo in case the legs need cleaning.
4. A tin of Johnson's Baby Powder. This is only needed after
   cleaning up has been done.
5. A grooming glove.
6. A fine-toothed comb.
7. A show lead.
8. Cotton wool and a bottle of boracic water to wipe the eyes.
9. A bottle of water for drinking and a bowl.
10. Another bowl if food is to be given at the show.
11. An apron for the exhibitor.
12. Either Vetzyme or bits of meat or whatever makes the dog
    show best.
13. A few dog biscuits to while away the hours.
14. A dog coat if it is winter, for the hall may be draughty.

These are the basic needs for a day at a show. If it is raining
the dog should be coated for the journey and the entry into the
show, then if it is cold in the hall the dry coat can be put on.
There are some excellent pantaloons in mackintosh on the
market which come right down to the feet and these do save a
tremendous amount of dirt.

If the dog is at all prone to car sickness an anti-sickness pill
should be given before setting off.

The next thing is to buy a catalogue and find out where
Cavaliers are benched. Having found your bench, settle the
young hopeful in on his blanket and remove the collar and
lead. This is most important, as a dog may otherwise get
caught up in its lead or collar and can strangle. In fact this did
happen to a pug at a show.

It is more than possible that this new and strange behaviour is going to be thought very odd by the newcomer to the show ring. If the puppy has been taken around by its owner in the local town it will be far less alarmed than one who has hardly met any strangers. A cringing creature in the ring is no joy to look at and certainly won't win a prize. Equally so, an over-boisterous dog, jumping up the whole time, won't have much chance, as the judge will be unable to assess its merits. Naturally any judge makes allowances for a young puppy, for it cannot be expected to behave like an experienced veteran.

The normal procedure in Cavaliers, although each judge may vary slightly, is to take a quick look in general at all the dogs lined up and then walk them all around in a circle. Having done a couple of circles, the judge will have each individual dog up on the table and go over it. This means that the dog must be trained to stand well on a table. Having examined it thoroughly on the table the exhibit will be asked to walk up and down or possibly in a triangle. When all the entrants in that class have been individually examined they will be asked to spread out and make their dog stand to its best advantage. This is where the tricky part comes in. Cavaliers are rather prone to enjoy sitting down, which of course is not going to help at all. It may come to the point where the owner has to go down on hands and knees and set the dog up and see that it stays there. This is an uncomfortable position as well as rather inelegant, and it is far easier to persuade your dog to show naturally. This may take time, but a little care at the beginning will pay large dividends in the end.

Obviously a dog cannot stand to attention the whole time, therefore let it relax while the judge is looking at the other exhibits, but as soon as the eagle eye is anywhere near you attract the dog's attention and make it stand. This is where the Vetzyme or titbits come into use. Sometimes a crackle of paper or a quiet word will do the trick, but whatever tricks are used the attention of the dog must be obtained and held. To do this you must concentrate entirely on your dog and let everything else go out of your mind. Always keep the dog between you and the judge and, if possible, broadside on so that the outline may be seen.

There are many people who go into the show ring and if they

don't win at once give the whole thing up in a pet. If you are not prepared to be a good loser there is little point in entertaining the thought of showing. After all, it's a game of chance as well as skill, and anyone who thinks they will make a little fortune out of dog breeding is, I'm afraid, sadly mistaken.

In Cavaliers it may well take five to six years really to 'get somewhere' in the show and breeding world. It may be that your first purchase is a 'flyer' and goes to the top at once; this must be taken as great good luck and not the normal run of events. By saying that it takes time to get to the top I am in no way implying that a judge will give the high awards to the established breeders just because they are known, but it must stand to reason that anyone who has been a long time in the breed has gained much experience in the art of showing, presentation, and also of breeding the right dog to the right bitch. Therefore what they do present is probably better than the complete novice.

Any established breeder will always try to sell a good show specimen to the intending exhibitor, but it is then largely up to them to make the best of what they've got. Unfortunately there is always jealousy in every breed and if some uncomplimentary remarks are made about your exhibit it may be in a way a back-handed compliment. No one really bothers very much about a thoroughly bad dog and it could be just envy for a rather good specimen that is causing the comments.

It is not a wise move to take a bitch in season to a show. There are various reasons for this. For one thing it causes chaos if the class is a mixed one and dogs are present in the ring and for another thing a bitch in season will very often move badly, so not only do you jeopardize your own chances but also those of the other exhibitors, thereby making yourself unpopular. One other very good reason is that even if the classes are divided into dogs and bitches you may easily be benched next to a dog and that may upset him right from the word go.

Try to arrive at a show with plenty of time in hand. A mad rush through the venue, a hasty clean-up and then straight into the ring is not conducive to make your dog show well. It may well be that you will have to settle down and dry and clean him or her up if the weather is inclement. This takes time and the featherings must dry before they look anything at all.

Cavaliers, being a long-coated breed, need more attention than, say, a dachshund, in the cleaning-up process. Whereas with the smooth coats you can rub hard and they'll look all right quite shortly, with a Cavalier they must be combed thoroughly all over. The eyes should be gently wiped with the boracic water to erase any 'Cavalier tears' and the hair around the eyes must be dry. A light show lead is better than an ordinary collar and lead and will not disturb the hair so much.

Finally one word of warning. There are many unscrupulous people in the world today and it is never safe to leave your purse for a moment. I have even known purses to be taken out of people's pockets. There are always other exhibitors who you know sitting around the ring and they are always only too pleased to guard your purse for you while you are in the ring, and you can then return the kindness by guarding theirs when their turn comes.

A typical Cavalier
puppy at four weeks

K. B. Eachus

Cavaliers working in the River Avon, Wiltshire

C. M. Cooke

Miss P. M. Mayhew judges Ch. Hillbarn Alexander of Ttiweh (Blenheim), shown by Mrs Brita White, and Ch. Gabbs Sonday Tricolour), shown by Mrs L. Gardiner

C. M. Cooke

Rev. D. Lindsey Smith judges Ch. Mimi of Eyeworth (Blenheim), shown by the author, and Ch. Cerdric of Ttiweh (Blenheim), shown by Mrs A. Pitt

Swedish and
Danish Champion
Stormkappans
Darling (Blenheim)

Australian Champion
Moerangi Capsicum
(Tricolour)

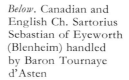

Below. Canadian and
English Ch. Sartorius
Sebastian of Eyeworth
(Blenheim) handled
by Baron Tournaye
d'Asten

Ch. Homerbrent Captivation (Tricolour)

F. E. *Garwood*/*Dog World*

Ch. Mintrode Jotham of Maxholt (Tricolour)

10

Cavaliers Abroad

THERE are now many recognized Cavalier Clubs outside the United Kingdom in America, Canada, Sweden, Finland, Eire, New Zealand and Australia but there are Cavaliers in most parts of the world. I have tried to track down as much information as possible about all these dogs, but I apologize if some have been omitted for it will be because I know nothing of them.

All the Cavalier owners, wherever they may be, are all very much one big Club. They all take a great interest in the activities of the breeders in other countries and are more than generous in sending special trophies for the various shows. The English parent club has also given trophies abroad. All the stock in all the countries has come from England originally and the fact that so many do so well in Variety and the Best-in-Show ring reflects a great credit on our English breeders regarding the quality that has been exported. As the standard is basically the same in all the countries this creates a great bond, and breeders reading our critiques in the English dog papers know exactly what is meant by the various terms used.

As the American Club is the largest overseas we will start our tour there.

America
The Club there was formed in 1956 by Mrs W. L. Lyons Brown and consisted of three members. I sent Mrs Brown over a small Black/Tan dog, Mercury of Eyeworth, as a present in 1952 when there were only five Cavaliers in the country. She then imported two bitches from me and both she and her husband became quite devoted to the breed. She remained in office until about 1962 and did a great deal to further the interest that

is now felt all over the States. In fact she was the pioneer of making Cavaliers known in America.

Cavaliers as such are not, much to the distress of most breeders in this country, recognized as a separate breed by the American Kennel Club. This is mainly due to the wishes of the ruling body of the American Cavalier Club, as there are now sufficient registrations, the records are well kept and there is high quality in the dogs shown. All the shows have been well run and highly successful, and indeed the A.K.C. would be happy to recognize the breed if the members so wished. Let us hope that soon our breed will take its place amongst the 'greats' recognized by the A.K.C.

In October 1982 there were 4,176 dogs, including imports, registered with the American Cavalier King Charles Spaniel Club, and there are 15 American Champions. At the moment, as well as the parent Club there are three Regional Clubs, one in the Midwest, one in the South, one in the North East, and there is another in the formative stage in the far West. So it can be seen that Cavaliers range right across America with Louisville still the centre of the breed. All the records are ably kept there by the Recording Secretary, Mrs J. J. Albrecht. They have their own Championship system based on wins at the National and Regional Shows. The Tri-State Cavalier Club was formed in 1971 by Dr and Mrs Jerome Roseff, who made up the first Ruby bitch in Cavaliers anywhere in the world into a Champion in Canada. She was Digers Red Ridinghood of Eyeworth and was exported by me to the Roseffs. Unfortunately the Roseffs do not play such a large part in Cavaliers nowadays.

Miss Elizabeth Spalding, whose Pargeter Fergus of Kilspindie, imported by her from the late Mrs Keswick, became the first dog from the States to be a Canadian Champion (and who also owned the first U.S. Cavalier Obedience Champion, Miss Edna of Mancross), still plays a very big part in the breed there. Mrs Albrecht, who as Mrs Garvin Brown also played a large part in the breed, continues to do so today and many of the Club Speciality Shows are held at her lovely home just outside Louisville, Kentucky.

The parent Club holds one of these shows a year and has

honoured our breeders by asking them to officiate on many occasions. The late Mrs Keswick was the judge in 1963, which was the Club's first show; I was the judge in 1964, the late Miss B. Sadler in 1965, the late Mrs Pitt in 1968, the late Mrs Daphne Murray in 1969 and Mrs Burgess in 1970. In 1966 at the show held at Mrs Burden's house on Long Island, the Club was lucky enough to have the privilege of Mr Alva Rosenberg as their judge. He was widely considered to be the best judge in the U.S.A., so the Club was rightly thrilled at being able to obtain his services. Since 1970 a succession of very well known English specialist judges have been asked to adjudicate. In 1974 Mrs Judy de Casembroot, the well known all-rounder and judge of Supreme Best in Show at Crufts, was the judge. There are too many names to mention individually as here we are in 1983. The entry of dogs has increased yearly and I am sure will continue to do so.

Cavaliers have done a lot of winning in miscellaneous classes at shows in many parts of the States as well as in this country. We wish them every success and hope that they continue with their wins. The Cavalier owners are a very dedicated band and travel literally thousands of miles to attend their Speciality Shows; nowadays with the Regional Clubs it does give owners more chance to exhibit their dogs under many different judges.

Canada
The breed is classified separately in this country and is called the Cavalier King Charles Spaniel. (The King Charles Spaniels are called English Toy Spaniels, as in the U.S.A.) Again their Standard is identical to the one that we use and the club formed by Mr Enrico Beneditti has, as far as I can find out, over 200 members.

According to the records the first Cavalier imported into the country was Deanhill Panda in 1956, registered in 1957. He was bred by Lady Ivor Spencer-Churchill and sent out to her brother, Mr C. Cunningham, in Toronto. In 1957 Mrs Stibbard from Ontario imported a Blenheim, Heatherside Belinda, and the Tricolour Hillbarn Ulysses, and also in 1957 Miss Carolyn Whitehead, now the wife of the famous English conductor, David Lloyd Jones, imported Augustus of Brandy-note into Quebec. In 1959 the Cunninghams imported a Tricolour bitch from Lady Ivor to mate with Panda and the first litter was born in October 1959.

The breed was first recognized by the Canadian Kennel Club in 1957, and by all accounts the future of the breed is a very rosy one and will become even more so when the American Kennel Club gives its recognition. It is difficult to pioneer a breed in Canada unless it is recognized in the U.S.A., although the majority of Canadians would not agree with this as they are enjoying the controlled growth of the breed and are regularly complimented by their judges on the increased quality of Canadian Cavaliers. Several Canadians cross the U.S. border for the Club Shows and have done exceedingly well in their classes. People want something that can be shown in both of these countries. There have been further successes lately, with Canadian and Bermudan Champion Newforest Rufus becoming the first Cavalier to win a Best in Show at an all Breed Show, and with Mrs Konkle and Mrs Lister both winning obedience titles with their dogs. There have also been up until 1981, two further Best in Show Cavaliers in Canada: Dr and Mrs Roseff's Ch. Digers Chandlers Snow Knight in 1979 and Ch. Azorese Mystiques Jolly twice in 1980 (now owned by Elaine Mitchell). Mrs Konkle has had two Canadian Companion Dogs titles and there are at least four CDX (Companion Dog Excellent).

There are now over 200 Canadian Champions. In Canada a dog must accumulate 10 points under at least three different judges. The Cavalier King Charles Spaniel Club of Canada has held Speciality Championship Shows for well over six years under many well known judges, including R. William Taylor who judged Cavaliers at Crufts in 1981 and the Toy Group in 1982, and Nigel Aubrey-Jones also well known in England. Mr Purser from Ontario is in the process of compiling a Canadian Champions book such as we have here, and I am sure we all wish him luck.

Eire

The Irish Club was formed in 1959 and had its first members' show in 1965 at Mrs S. Gainsford St Lawrence's beautiful property, Howth Castle, Dublin.

They held their first Championship Show in 1971. Since 1 January 1978, a Green Star system of points has been adopted for all Championship Shows at which Green Stars are offered in the breed. The one, three and four-point Green Star Certificate, awarded pre-1978, has been withdrawn and a new certificate showing the number of points won at each show has been substituted.

Under the new Green Star system an index figure is allocated to each sex, also to mixed dog and bitch classes. This index figure is arrived at by dividing the total number of valid exhibits at Championship Shows by the number of shows at which Green Stars were offered, during the previous year ending 30 June, in that breed. If there were no mixed classes in that year, ending 30 June, then the index figure will be ascertained by adding together the dog and bitch index figures.

Where the total number of eligible exhibits actually shown (in the dog, bitch, or mixed classes as the case may be) is equal to the index figure, then five Green Star points will be awarded. For every twenty per cent below the index figure, one point will be deducted and for every twenty per cent above, one will be added. All Green Star points are rounded up or down to the nearest whole number. For example:

Index fig.	Eligible exhibits shown	Green Star points
8	8	5
8	11	7
8	5	3

All Green Stars will have a value of between one and ten points and the Annual Champion requires thirty points.

To become an Irish Champion a dog must win Green Stars which total in value forty points. This total must include not less than 4×5-points won under four different judges. Dogs disqualified for any reason cannot be awarded Green Stars. This is a rather complicated sounding business, but one that no doubt can be easily got used to.

There are now forty-five Irish Champions and ten English and Irish Champions. Three of the Champions came from one litter bred by Lady Levinge, and seventeen of the Champions are owned or bred by Mrs Nugent, five of them being out of her Tnegun Florabell. One Champion is Miss Turle's and Mrs Bartel's Sunninghill Perseus of Loch Fee, who is the sire of Heatherbell, Patsy and Perte, the first bitch champions.

Cavaliers in Eire, where there was once only a very small Club, now regularly have the highest entry in the Toy Group, and are, as in the United Kingdom, gaining in popularity. Mrs Nugent is the popular Chairman of the Club, but alas with the high cost of travel Irish exhibitors are slightly curtailed in their showing activities in the U.K. However, it is not too difficult to send a bitch over to England by air for mating and then back again.

Holland

Cavaliers are quite a popular breed in Holland, as indeed they certainly should be with their history so tied up with that of the country.

By far the largest breeder was Mme Van den Boom of the 'Fanfare' kennels. She imported three dogs and five bitches from England who were the foundation of her kennel. They all became champions in many countries and their offspring have started off many smaller kennels. She was a very regular show-goer and was always in the front line with her dogs in all the European countries that she visited. Mme Gerth van Heukelom of the Caballero Cavaliers was the next biggest breeder. She imported two dogs and two bitches and has done a lot of successful breeding and showing. She now lives in this country. There are various other smaller breeders in Holland who have had success both in showing and breeding. On 11 October 1981 the Cavalier Club Nederland was formed. Club membership grew rapidly in 1982 from 50 to 400 members.

Madame Van den Boom no longer breeds or shows Cavaliers but is Patron of the Club. The first Club Show was held on 19 September 1982 and judged by Mrs D. Fry (Amantra) with an all time record number of entries for Cavaliers in Holland – 128. There are now approximately 2000 Cavaliers registered in Holland with 39 Champions up to 1981.

All the four colours are judged collectively on the Continent, apart from Germany, about which more in the German section.

There is only one C.A.C.I.B. awarded at the shows. This stands for *Certificat d'Aptitude au Championat International de Beauté* and is offered at all Continental shows which come under the *Fédération Cynologique Internationale.* To become an International Champion abroad a dog must win four C.A.C.I.B.s in three countries under three different judges, a much harder task than we have over here in every way.

It is possible in the British Isles to make a dog an international champion without it having gone out of the quarantine area. To do this it must, as stated under 'Eire' heading, be both an English Champion and an Irish Champion and in Ireland must abide by the Irish Kennel Club rules regarding Green Stars.

The shows are spaced far apart which entails a great deal of travelling and great expense, and very often bad weather conditions. To be awarded the first C.A.C.I.B. the dog must be fifteen months old and then twelve months must elapse before he can win his second one. In Holland four C.C.s are needed to become a Dutch Champion under at least two different judges and to win the qualifying one the dog must be twenty-seven months old. The C.A.C.s won at the Winner Show in Amsterdam count for two. Belgium needs three C.C.s under two different judges to become a Belgian Champion and there must be an interval of twelve months between the first and last.

As can be seen, all these countries have different qualifications for their National Champions, but to become an Int. Ch. the rules of the F.C.I. must be adhered to.

It all sounds very complicated to the ordinary English breeder, but I am assured by the residents in these various countries that you get so used to it that it becomes second nature. This seems hard to believe, but must obviously be the case.

It seems that Cavaliers are definitely on the increase in Holland and quite a few of our English Toy all-rounders have been asked to judge over there.

Great hospitality is always shown to our English judges and I've not met one who hasn't enjoyed him- or herself enormously.

Germany

There is nothing like the interest in Germany shown in Cavaliers as there is in Holland, although they are scheduled at most of the big shows. There the colours are classified separately and at five or six special shows a year each colour is awarded a separate ticket. Three of these tickets are needed to become a German Champion.

Frau Bernhard of Oldenburg imported Vesper of Sunninghill, who is an Int. and German Champion and a successful sire.

There are two regular show-going kennels who have been successful, but have no English imports. They are Gräfin Luise Zu Erbach Fürstenau from Hessen and Frau Pfeiffer from Stegen.

Most of the Dutch breeders make the trek into Germany for the big shows, and quite a trek it is at times. Mrs Murray exported two dogs to Germany from this country, so that may have helped to swell the interest in them.

France

In December 1982 Cavaliers were still included in a four Toy Spaniel Breed Club – Pekingese, Japanese Chin, King Charles Spaniels and Cavaliers. The rule of the Société Centrale Canine (like our Kennel Club) is that it only grants a breed its own separate club when they have had at least 100 puppies a year for two years. At the end of 1982 the Cavaliers in France reached 200 puppies so I hope that by now they have their own Club. The leading light in Paris has been Madame Raymonde Dufourg, who indeed owns a Champion. Mme Chevallereau from Livilliers in France is also prominent in the breed. They have imported dogs from Switzerland where there is no club but several Cavalier breeders including Mme Guyot Claudine who has been breeding for about eight years.

The French owners exhibit their dogs regularly in their own country, Luxembourg, Belgium and Monaco. I am sure that we all wish them every success with the founding of their own Club.

Italy

While on the Continent a word must be said about Italy. There are two Italian Champions, one is Carlo of Kormar, who was made up in July 1965. He is a Black and Tan bred by Miss Marshall and owned by Miss Marta Carpanelli. I myself met this little dog quite by chance while I was in Venice a few years ago. Miss Carpanelli is an enthusiastic exhibitor and takes Carlo to most of the shows.

There are also several pets which have been exported to Italy but not shown.

A little Ruby also went to Italy at the same time as Carlo from Miss Marshall, but seems to have found its way to Japan via Italy!

It is a pity that the breed is not more common in Italy as it is so near the land of its origin.

New Zealand

Cavaliers have done extremely well in New Zealand. They are a very popular breed and have done very well in winning State classes at the big shows and also the top awards, as will be seen by a more detailed account which follows.

Distances are enormous for the little band of pioneers who travel as many shows as they can manage, and it is great credit to them that so many Cavaliers are seen at so many of the big shows.

Mrs Grocott and Mr and Mrs D. Montfort are without doubt the biggest breeders.

Cavaliers were first brought to New Zealand by Mr Antony St John who went out to that country to farm. His mother sent out a breeding pair to him from England, but unfortunately before they arrived he hurt his back and had to leave his farm and go to the town for treatment. Someone had told him that

Mrs Grocott would quarantine these two dogs for him and so he duly approached her. Mrs Grocott had never seen a Cavalier and thought they were some kind of funny little dog between a King Charles and a Peke. However, she agreed to take them for the time being. These two little dogs were Antony of Avoncliffe and Mingshang Sarah. Mr St John then decided to move to Canada, and having tried and failed to get someone else to take the Cavaliers, Mrs Grocott agreed to keep them until they were sent for and to breed a litter to help pay the expenses. This litter was born in 1950 and was the starting of the breed in New Zealand. Antony of Avoncliffe received his Championship Certificate in September 1952, but was never placed in variety, mainly because none of the judges knew how good he was. In October 1952 Mrs Grocott took Moerangi Mistress to the Royal Show at Hawkes Bay where she won the Toy Puppy Stakes, Toy Novice Stakes and Best Toy Puppy. Not a bad beginning for a little-known breed. It was at this show that Miss Brodie first became interested in the breed and shortly afterwards started to import from England.

A great help to the breed in New Zealand was the fact that Sir Charles Madden went out from this country with Lady Madden to be Chief of Naval Staff and Lady Madden took with her her Cavalier, Patch of Little Stream. This little bitch was mated to Antony of Avoncliffe and had two bitch puppies. Antony and Mistress also were mated and produced four puppies, one of which was bought by Miss Brodie and was called Moerangi Wee Willie Winkie.

In 1955 Mrs Keswick exported Pargeter Pennypost to Mrs Grocott and the following year he was first in the Toy Stakes. In the same year Wee Willie Winkie was Reserve Best Toy at the Second National Show. Also in this year Miss Brodie imported Pargeter Elegance, a Ruby bitch, and the following year the Tricolour Deanhill Jolly Roger, bred by Lady Ivor Spencer-Churchill. In 1958 Roger was Best Toy and Reserve Best in Show at Danneyirke. In 1959 a daughter of his was best Junior in Show.

So, slowly but surely, the breed was gaining a foothold. That same year the Ruby, Merry Musketeer of Eyeworth, went out from me and in 1960 Angelo of Crustadele went to Mrs

Grocott and after that my Eyeworth Professor Higgins, whose daughter went to Perth and was Best Puppy Bitch in Show. In 1964 Pargeter Memento arrived and at his first show was Reserve Best in Show.

A Club was formed called the Tiki Cavalier King Charles Spaniel Club, and the New Zealanders paid the parent country a great compliment by asking Mrs Keswick to be their Patroness.* Mrs Grocott, who has been largely instrumental in getting the Club started, is kind enough to say how grateful they all are to the English breeders who have sent out good honest stock. The breed has definitely established itself and by 1979 there were five Clubs in New Zealand, all of which seem to be thriving. I judged the Cavalier Championship Shows in both South and North Islands in 1978, where I found the quality very high.

Australia

Cavaliers have only been in Australia since 1960. They were pioneered by Mrs R. Esler, who unfortunately later broke her back and had to get rid of her Cavaliers. The then Governor-General of Australia, Lord de Lisle, had two Cavaliers out there, but on his return to England they came with him, and were not bred from out there.

There have been many imports from New Zealand and quite a few dogs have been imported from England, in spite of the long sea journey. They can, however, now be sent by air. Each state in Australia has its own Canine Association, but it is only in certain states that Cavaliers appear in the registrations. There is a Club now in New South Wales (of which I am Patron) which boasts of over 100 members and well over 300 dogs registered; they have held shows and done much to further the breed in this country. Mrs Hendry is very much a leading light in this Club, together with Mrs Leach, and she has made up many champions, including Ch. Gaysprite the Regent who is the only Cavalier in New South Wales to win an All Breed show. Mrs Hendry purchased her first Cavalier from

*After her death the Club paid my husband the honour of asking him to be their Patron.

Miss Reading and travelled over 2,000 miles to meet her and the dogs. Obviously to be a dog lover in Australia you mustn't mind travelling!

Tasmania has Cavalier classes and Ch. Gaysprite Pandora has won three Toy Groups there. Western Australia is Miss Reading's province and she has done much to further the breed there and to make up champions. Miss Reading and Mrs Paterson bought their first puppy in 1962. They also purchased a son of New Zealand Ch. Eyeworth Professor Higgins and took him to the Melbourne Royal Show where he won Best of Breed.

There are examinations for potential judges and several of the Cavalier breeders have passed these exams, thereby enabling the breed to be judged by someone who understands them. Many of our English all-rounders place Cavaliers in the Variety classes, and Mr David Roche gave a Cavalier Best Open dog and Best Toy just after he returned from England.

I also judged the Sydney Championship Show in 1978 and found very high quality and very large entries. Ch. Chandlers King Midas, belonging to Dennis Montford and bred by Mrs Preece in England, continues to be the leading stud dog. When I made him Best in Show in 1978 I think he was the best Ruby I had ever seen and he had an equally beautiful young son, who was unfortunately poisoned (and died) by an unscrupulous interloper in the kennels who also administered the poison to King Midas, but he was lucky enough to recover.

The New South Wales Club now has a Rescue Service which does a very good job. Their President, Mrs Jeannie Montford, is a great leading light and together with her husband, Mrs Massey and Mr Carpenter, does stalwart work with the Year Book. The breed is thriving and Mrs Grocott is often to be seen judging in this country as well as America and Canada.

Sweden

This country has gone from strength to strength. In 1966 there was a total of 126 Cavaliers registered with the Swedish Kennel Club, but in 1971 there were 519, so for the total period of 1961–71 there have been 1,726 registered. During the same period there have been sixty-one champions made up in

Sweden. Of these twenty-five were imported from England or Holland, and of the thirty-six Swedish-bred champions nine were sired by International and Nordic Ch. Kingmaker of Ttiweh, four by Ch. Festival of Sunninghill, four by Ch. Hillbarn Ian, three by International and Nordic Ch. Stormkappans Joker, three by Ch. Welland Valley Solomon, two by Int. Belgian and German Ch. Fanfare for Romeo, and two by Ch. Backtimjans Claro. Kingmaker has also two champion sons in Finland and one in Holland which is owned by Madame van den Boom – and Joker has sired the first (as yet) home-bred Champion in Norway. He is Ch. Cinzano and was bred by Mrs Elizabeth Oksas. There seems to be a growing interest in Cavaliers in Norway and there have been some exports there from Sweden as well as from England. Mrs Grete Otterbeck has had two litters and has imported McGoogans Royal George of Hillhurst who has at least one C.C.

Mrs Östergren was certainly the biggest breeder in the country and her Stormkappans Prefix has had some spectacular wins. Her Int. and Nordic Ch. Stormkappans Joker was Best Toy at the Norwegian Kennel Club show in Tonsberg, Norway in November 1966, and her Stormkappans Darling at fifteen months was a Champion with six certificates, and in 1966 was Best of Breed at the Swedish Kennel Club's International Show, winning over three champions while still only fifteen months old. Mrs Svensson and Mrs Ausma Lume are also big breeders.

Up to date Cavaliers are the second biggest (and maybe now the top) Toy Breed in Sweden as one can see from the registration figure of four in 1961, which jumped to 1,060 in 1976; but they also have had big wins at the International shows in Norway, Sweden and Finland. Int. and Nordic Ch. Stormkappans Zombie owned by Mr and Mrs Begquist and bred by Mrs Östergren was Best Toy at an International All Breeds show in Norway in 1974.

The first Black/Tan and Ruby Champions, owned by Mrs Peterséu, were Ch. Slyuana of Restoria and Ch. Dondiego of Kormar. There are two more Ruby Champions now: Ch. Pantisa Willy Wagtail and Harskas Isabell, both of whom were made up in 1974.

The first B/T to win a Toy Group was Swedish and Finnish Ch. Jung Fältets Toddie, owned by Mrs Ledih and bred by Mrs E. Jungefact. This was won at Ekenas in Finland in 1975.

At the International K.C. Show in Stockholm in 1974 Mrs Östergren's group of five home-bred dogs and bitches went Best Group in Show. The first time ever, and a *very* good effort.

A Club has been formed and has very good support. In 1973 Mrs Pitt judged their second club show and had a marvellous entry. They are a breed society which is growing rapidly and with quality. Mrs Östergren has written an extremely good book on Cavaliers in Sweden; from the reports that I have had from English judges in Sweden, the quality is extremely high. I also hear that there is a small but active Finnish Club recently formed but I have no details.

Norway

There were forty-nine registrations in 1976 making a total of 224 from 1961. There are seven Norwegian owned Champions and three of them are Norwegian bred, two imported from England and two from Sweden. Two Cavaliers have won the Toy Group which is a great honour with such a small community, one bred by Mrs Östergren and one by Mrs Gillis in England.

Mexico

This is a new break-through and proving rather a difficult one. Señor Alejandro Rojas has a Blenheim Int. Mexican Champion imported from Mrs Östergren and he also owns another Int. Mexican Champion. In all there are twenty-three Cavaliers in that country.

South Africa

Way back in 1959 Miss Devis had four South African Champions, but, as she herself said, with no competition it would be possible to make almost any Cavalier a champion. Gigue of Knightlow, bred by Mrs Barnett, went from this country to become a champion, also Nestor of Ttiweh, bred by Mrs Pitt. In 1959 four Cavaliers in all went from this country to the Union and two went to Southern Rhodesia.

The judges did not know much about the breed and were frightened of putting them up. Miss Devis did breed quite a few litters, but they have all disappeared into obscurity. In 1966 there were only two champions alive in that country as far as was known – Mrs J. Boyd's Ch. Isobel of Little Breach, a Blenheim imported from Mrs L. R. Percival, and Mr W. B. Campbell-Martin's Marrakesh's Melchior of Kormar, a Black/Tan dog bred by Miss Marshall who is by Ch. Aloysius of Sunninghill. These two were mated together and produced a Black/Tan and Ruby litter. One of this litter went to Rhodesia where there was a possibility that it might be shown, but the others all went to pet homes.

At the moment there are two fairly new breeders of Cavaliers in the Union, Mr and Mrs T. G. L. Lawson from the Transvaal, who now live in Somerset West. They bought two bitches, Kaytee and Marina, from Mrs Jean Boyd. Marina is out of Cornelius of Rhosnessney, whose mother was my Sugar of Eyeworth and Great Grandfather Ch. Clarion of Eyeworth. Kaytee's grandfather is Ch. Marrakesh's Melchior of Kormar. These two bitches are now S.A. Champions and Kaytee's litter sister is knocking at the door. The Lawsons have now imported a dog from Mrs Coaker, Homerbrent Revocation, who just two weeks before arriving in the Union won the C.C. and Best of Breed at Paignton, and up to date has won twenty-two Best of Breeds, eleven C.C.s and one Reserve C.C., and went Best in Show at the Toy Breeders Association Championship Show. His crowning achievement was to go third in Show out of an entry of 560 dogs at the Northern Free State Kennel Club Championship Show in the Orange Free State.

The Kennel Union of South Africa say that there were only 72 Cavaliers registered in the Union in 1981. There are a number of new owners particularly in the Transvaal. Dr Sandra Nievwoudt of Schweizer-Keneke has a number of show dogs and is a constant entrant at most shows countrywide.

Mr George McCann of Johannesburg has two Cavaliers, one of which is a Champion bred by Mr Lawson. Other people who try to get Cavaliers noticed in South Africa by showing and breeding are Mr and Mrs Shears, Mr and Mrs Peter Hutchinson (who did very well with their Ch. Black Isle's Dawn) and in Natal Miss de Jager has a handsome Blenheim,

Ch. Black Isle's Fabian who has done very well in the show ring.

Unfortunately most of the puppies bred are sold as pets. There is no Club in South Africa, and at the moment there seems little likelihood of one being formed.

Two Blenheims went to Zimbabwe in 1965 to help swell the tiny band that was already there. These were a dog Beau Sabreur of Eyeworth and a bitch Dulceria of Pield. Their owner, Mrs R. M. Walters, had already shown them and a certain amount of interest seemed to be shown in the breed. Included among the other known Cavaliers in Zimbabwe is S.A. Champion Pepe's Major of Black Isle. By 1979 Zimbabwe was trying very hard and Mrs Clarke was pushing ahead with her imports. Mr and Mrs Alex Ingleby do their best by continuing to show when possible.

REGISTRATION TOTALS AT KENNEL CLUB

1946	10	1966	2124
1947	181	1967	2352
1948	183	1968	2638
1949	231	1969	2899
1950	314	1970	3192
1951	310	1971	3562
1952	352	1972	4471
1953	279	1973	5071
1954	380	1974	5795
1955	450	1975	5407
1956	523	1976	2501
1957	588	1977	1887
1958	724	1978	5509
1959	883	1979	8771
1960	1150	1980	8898
1961	1235	1981	8530
1962	1595	1982	8927
1963	1556	(up to	
1964	1794	November)	
1965	1864		

BREED CLUBS

Cavalier King Charles Spaniel Club
  Hon Sec: Mrs D. Maclaine, The Grove, Mundon, Maldon, Essex
Three Counties Pekingese and Cavalier Society
  Hon Sec: Mrs B. M. Blackmore, Jasmine Cottage, Horton, Wem,
  Salop
Scottish Cavalier King Charles Spaniel Club
  Hon Sec: Mr George Donaldson, Viewfield, 112 Main Street,
  Larbert, FK5 3LA
Cavalier King Charles Spaniel Club of Ireland
  Hon Sec: Mrs Rita O'Daly, Ferndale, Kiltale, Dunsany, Co.
  Meath, Eire
West of England Cavalier King Charles Spaniel Club
  Hon Sec: Mrs D. Fry, 'Tall Timbers', Summers Lane, Knightcott,
  Banwell, Avon
Northern Cavalier King Charles Spaniel Society
  Hon Sec: Miss B. M. Henshaw, The Orchard, Wharf Lane,
  Sedgwick, Kendall, Cumbria, LA8 0JW
Midland Cavalier King Charles Spaniel Club
  Hon Sec: Mrs F. Stewart, Leigh Court, Nr. Worcester, WR6 5LB
Eastern Counties Cavalier King Charles Spaniel Society
  Hon Sec: Mr E. M. J. Tweddell, 45 Parklands Avenue, Shipham,
  Norfolk
Northern Ireland Cavalier King Charles Spaniel Club
  Hon Sec: Mrs B. Megarry, 21 Victoria Road, Ballyhalbert,
  Co. Down
Southern Cavalier King Charles Spaniel Club
  Hon Sec: Mrs J. Wright, 198 Connaught Road, Brookwood,
  Woking, Surrey, GU24 0AH
The South and West Wales Cavalier King Charles Spaniel Club
  Hon Sec: Mrs B. Snape, 173 Elan Way, Caldicot, Newport, Gwent
Cavalier King Charles Spaniel Club U.S.A.
  Hon Sec: Dr Charles Plank, 240 E30 Street Apt. 1C, New York,
  NY 10016

Cavaliers of the Northeast
  Hon Sec: Mrs Reginald H. Fullerton Jr, The Dormers, Watch Hill, RI 02891, U.S.A.
Cavaliers of the South
  Hon Sec: Mr George Quinn, Jr, 1111 Strong St., Madison, AL 35758, U.S.A.
Cavaliers of the Midwest
  Hon Sec: Mrs Patricia M. Dye, 2528 Bolton, St. Charles, MO 63301, U.S.A.
Tiki Cavalier King Charles Spaniel Club
  Hon Sec: Mrs D. Bell, 2/136 St. Andrews Road, Auckland 5, New Zealand
East Coast Cavalier King Charles Spaniel Club
  Hon Sec: Mrs M. Tolley, P.O. Box 3005, Mahora, Hastings, N.Z.
Central Cavalier & King Charles Spaniel Club
  Hon Sec: David McCullough, 90 Hewer Crescent, NaeNae, N.Z.
Canterbury Cavalier King Charles Spaniel Club
  Hon Sec: Mrs M. Wells, 24 Linwood Avenue, Christchurch 1, N.Z.
Otago-Southland Cavalier King Charles Spaniel Club
  Hon Sec: Mrs S. Ashby, 24 Ravenswood Road, St. Clair, Dunedin, N.Z.
Cavalier King Charles Spaniel Club of New South Wales
  Hon Sec: Mrs M. Madigan, 56 Austin Street, Lane Cove, NSW 2066, Australia
Cavalier King Charles Spaniel Club of Victoria
  Hon Sec: unknown
Cavalier King Charles Spaniel Club of Canada
  Membership Sec: Mrs Brigida Reynolds, 153 Garrard Road, Whitby, Ontario
Cavaliersallskapets
  Sec: Erna-Britt Nordin, Ronningsbergs 81800, VALBO, Sweden
Cavalier Club Nederland
  Sec: Mr B. M. Hilberts, Midden Woerd 37, 2671 DL Naaldwijk, Holland
Club Pekinois, Japonais, King Charles et Cavalier King Charles
  Sec (Cavaliers): Mme Chevallereau, 10 Rue du Moulin, Livilliers, 95300 Pontoise, France
Cavalier King Charles Spaniel Club of Finland
  Sec: unknown

CHAMPIONS TO 31 OCTOBER 1984

Name	Colour	Sex	Sire	Dam	Owner	Breeder	Date of Birth
1948							
Daywell Roger	Blenheim	D	Cannonhill Richey	Daywell Nell	Miss J. Pitt	Mrs L. Brierley	7.10.45
Amanda Loo of Ttiweh	Black/Tan	B	Bernard of Aston-Downs	Princess Anita De Fontenay	Mrs E. R. Burroughs	Mrs Mansour	11.6.46
Katrina of Loyalway	Blenheim	B	Bouncer Rupert	Gloria of Grenewich	Captain Spink	Mrs S. Massingham	17.8.46
1949							
Royalist of Veren	Black/Tan	D	Cannonhill Richey	Rustle of Veren	Breeder	Mrs V. Rennie	28.10.45
Harmony of Ttiweh	Blenheim	D	Ch. Daywell Roger	Ch. Litle Dorritt of Ttiweh	Breeder	Mrs A. Pitt	25.6.47
Hillbarn Alexander of Ttiweh	Blenheim	D	Ch. Daywell Roger	Cassandra of Hillbarn	Mrs B. S. White	Mrs H. Pilkington	26.4.47
Mingshang Sir Roger	Blenheim	D	Ch. Daywell Roger	Mingshang Sarah	Breeder	Miss P. Mayhew	4.8.47
1950							
Mingshang Corinna	Blenheim	B	Young Pretender of Grenewich	Annabelle of Astondowns	Mrs I. J. Green	Mrs H. Pilkington	1.3.46

Name	Colour	Sex	Sire	Dam	Owner	Breeder	Date of Birth
Jason of Ttiweh	Blenheim	D	Daywell Nimrod of Ttiweh	Discord of Ttiweh	Miss J. Pynsent	Miss A. Turner	11.10.48
Comfort of Ttiweh	Blenheim	B	Cannonhill Richey	Deborah of Avoncliffe	Mrs A. Pitt	Mrs L. Hitching	31.3.45
Little Dorrit of Ttiweh	Blenheim	B	Bouncer Rupert	Belinda of Saxham	Mrs A. Pitt	Mrs J. Eldred	14.11.45
Dolores of Hillbarn	Tricolour	B	Ch. Daywell Roger	Clarissa of Hillbarn	Breeder	Mrs H. Pilkington	15.2.48
Pargeter Jollyean of Avoncliffe	Blenheim	D	Ch. Daywell Roger	Avoncliffe Heatherbelle	Mrs D. Keswick	Mrs L. Hitching	21.5.47
Heatherside Fiona	Blenheim	B	Ch. Mingshang Sir Roger	Mingshang Caroline	Breeder	Mrs I. J. Green	16.9.48
1951 Trilby of Ttiweh	Blenheim	B	Ttiweh Prince Medor De Fontenay	Cinderella of Turnworth	Mrs O. E. Durrant	Miss J. Pitt	11.1.50
Claudette of Hillbarn	Tricolour	B	Young Pretender of Grenewich	Annabelle of Astondowns	Breeder	Mrs H. Pilkington	1.3.46
Jupiter of Ttiweh	Blenheim	D	Ch. Daywell Roger	Ch. Little Dorrit of Ttiweh	Breeder	Mrs A. Pitt	24.8.49
Mingshang Fabion	Blenheim	D	Ch. Mingshang Sir Roger	Mingshang Rosalind	Breeder	Miss P. M. Mayhew	2.11.49

	Colour		Sire	Dam	Breeder	Owner	Date
Felicity of Hillbarn	Tricolour	B	Ch. Hillbarn Desmond	Cassandra of Hillbarn	Breeder	Mrs H. Pilkington	8.7.49
Tiweh Flora of Mahnew	Blenheim	B	Veren Charles by Candlelight	Daywell Frances	Mrs E. Russell	Miss C. Wenham	7.8.49
1952 Hillbarn Desmond	Tricolour	D	Ch. Daywell Roger	Clarissa of Hillbarn	Breeder	Mrs H. Pilkington	15.2.48
Prologue of Ttiweh	Tricolour	B	Ch. Daywell Roger	Rowena of Aston-downs	Miss P. Murray	Col F. F. Deakin	31.1.50
Lucinda O'Cockpen	Tricolour	B	Ch. Harmony of Ttiweh	Crinoline by Candlelight	Lt Col H. G. C. Laird	Mrs R. Grant	15.6.50
Lady Be Good of Astondowns	Blenheim	B	Ronald of Aston-downs	Emerald De Fontenay	Mrs N. Compton	Mr V. Green	24.10.49
Linnett of Ttiweh	Blenheim	B	Daywell Nimrod of Ttiweh	Victoria of Ttiweh	Mrs C. Forbes	Mrs A. Pitt	25.3.49
1953 Juliet of Hillbarn	Tricolour	B	Hamlet of Ttiweh	Deborah of Hillbarn	Breeder	Mrs H. Pilkington	17.1.51
Pargeter Patron	Blenheim	D	Pargeter Athos	Pargeter Cliquot	Breeder	Mrs D. Keswick	8.11.50
Gabbs Sonday	Tricolour	B	Daywell Nell's Son	Carlotta of Loyaltway	Breeder	Mrs L. Gardiner	14.10.50
Piper of Goldicote	Blenheim	D	Pericles of Goldicote	Goldicote Jane	Mrs R. Pilkington	Mrs E. James	8.10.50

Name	Colour	Sex	Sire	Dam	Owner	Breeder	Date of Birth
Armourer of Ttiweh	Blenheim	D	Ttiweh Prince Medor De Fontenay	Candid of Ttiweh	Mrs A. Forbes	Mrs A. Pitt	11.6.50
Polka of Ttiweh	Blenheim	B	Ch. Daywell Roger	Ch. Lady Be Good of Astondowns	Mrs E. Barnett	Mrs A. Pitt	8.7.51
1954 Raoul of Ttiweh	Blenheim	D	Ch. Hillbarn Alexander of Ttiweh	Fickle of Ttiweh	Mrs L. White	Mrs D. J. Murray	7.10.51
Heatherside Anthea	Blenheim	B	Young Pretender of Grenewich	Daywell Amber	Breeder	Mrs I. J. Green	11.9.49
Hillbarn Kevin	Tricolour	D	Ch. Hillbarn Desmond	Ch. Claudette of Hillbarn	Breeder	Mrs H. Pilkington	7.3.51
Emerald of Astondowns	Tricolour	B	Hillbarn Ebenezer	Emerald De Fontenay	Mrs H. Pilkington	Mr V. Green	28.7.51
Heatherside Andrew	Blenheim	D	Young Pretender of Grenewich	Daywell Amber	Breeder	Mrs I. J. Green	11.9.49
Pargeter Thundercloud of Ttiweh	Black/Tan	D	Ch. Daywell Roger	Ch. Amanda Loo of Ttiweh	Mrs D. Keswick	Mrs A. Pitt	6.6.50
Matilda of Ttiweh	Blenheim	B	Ch. Daywell Roger	Rowena of Astondowns	Mrs Tupman	Col F. F. Deakin	7.3.51

Name	Colour	Sex	Sire	Dam	Breeder	Owner	Date
Ophelia of Tuweh	Blenheim	B	Hamlet of Tuweh	Araminta of Evenlode	Mrs M. Taylor	Miss J. Pitt	18.9.50
1955 Hillbarn Quixote	Tricolour	D	Ch. Heatherside Andrew	Ch. Felicity of Hillbarn	Breeder	Mrs H. Pilkington	23.5.53
Abelard of Tuweh	Blenheim	D	Mars of Tuweh	Rose Marie of Jelunga	Miss M. B. Sadler	Mrs A. Pitt	11.10.50
1956 Welland Valley Raoul's Son	Blenheim	D	Ch. Raoul of Tuweh	Victoria of Burgercroft	Mr and Mrs P. Tregoning	Miss G. Bass	20.10.53
Pargeter Phyllida	Blenheim	B	Ch. Pargeter Patron	Pargeter Phoebe	Breeder	Mrs D. Keswick	30.6.54
Pargeter Philander	Blenheim	D	Ch. Pargeter Patron	Pargeter Phoebe	Breeder	Mrs D. Keswick	30.6.54
Prunella of Hillbarn	Tricolour	D	Ch. Hillbarn Desmond	Ch. Dolores of Hillbarn	Breeder	Mrs H. Pilkington	11.11.52
Hillbarn Thomas	Blenheim	D	Ch. Hillbarn Quixote	Ch. Dolores of Hillbarn	Mrs B. S. White	Mrs H. Pilkington	4.6.55
Heatherside Petal	Blenheim	B	Ch. Heatherside Andrew	Doghill Petronella	Breeder	Mrs I. J. Green	30.6.54
1957 Pineridge Bridie	Blenheim	B	Shepheards Little Noddy	Hillbarn Perdita	Mrs Tupman	Mrs V. J. Couche	30.10.54

Name	Colour	Sex	Sire	Dam	Owner	Breeder	Date of Birth
Pineapple Poll of Ttiweh	Blenheim	B	Rafi of Crustadele	Ch. Prologue of Ttiweh	Mrs A. Pitt	Miss P. J. Murray	18.9.54
Aloysius of Sunninghill	Tricolour	D	Amulet of Sunninghill	Louisa of Sunninghill	Miss P. Turle	Mr G. P. Wilson	27.11.55
Niobe of Ttiweh	Blenheim	B	Sherriff of Ttiweh	Candid of Ttiweh	Lt Col H. G. C. Laird	Mrs A. Pitt	3.12.53
1958 Orlando of Goldicote	Blenheim	D	Peter of Astondowns	Bridgitt of Goldicote	Breeder	Mrs R. Pilkington	20.9.55
Unity of Hillbarn	Tricolour	B	Ch. Hillbarn Desmond	Renee of Hillbarn	Breeder	Mrs H. Pilkington	15.7.55
Welland Valley Lively	Blenheim	D	Ch. Heatherside Andrew	Pargeter Mimosa	Mrs I. J. Green	Mrs E. Petrie	23.7.55
Infantas Katherine of Eyeworth	Blenheim	B	Charles O'Cockpen	Patience of Goldicote	Lady Forwood	Miss R. Wansbrough	23.8.56
1959 Pargeter Polyantha of Goldicote	Blenheim	B	Ch. Orlando of Goldicote	Pargeter Philippa	Mrs D. Keswick	Mrs R. Pilkington	18.4.57
My Fair Lady of Eyeworth	Tricolour	B	Ch. Aloysius of Sunninghill	Carousel of Eyeworth	Breeder	Lady Forwood	14.10.58
Barings Elizabertha	Black/Tan	B	Royal Flush of Veren	Barings Araminta	Breeder	Mrs M. Patten	3.5.53

Name	Colour	Sex	Sire	Dam	Breeder	Owner	Date
Sunninghill Perseus of Loch Fee	Blenheim	D	Ch. Aloysius of Sunninghill	Perle of Lenharra	Miss P. Turle and Mrs M. H. Bartels	Mrs M. H. Bartels	7.8.57
Pargeter Anemone	Blenheim	B	Ch. Abelard of Ttuweh	Pargeter Fleur De Lys	Mrs D. Keswick	Miss M. B. Sadler	23.9.58
1960							
Yadipati of Goldicote	Blenheim	D	Joker of Goldicote	Bridgitt of Goldicote	Breeder	Mrs R. Pilkington	20.8.57
Clarion of Eyeworth	Tricolour	D	Chello of Eyeworth	Venus of Eyeworth	Breeder	Lady Forwood	26.3.57
Alisoun of Corvedell	Blenheim	B	Ch. Hillbarn Thomas	Garland of Corvedell	Miss S. White	Mrs B. S. White	12.4.58
Rekalb Julie	Tricolour	B	Sherriff of Ttuweh	Louise of Kempvale	Breeder	Mrs N. V. Blacker	29.11.54
White Collar Worker	Tricolour	D	Ch. Aloysius of Sunninghill	Melody of Eyeworth	Breeder	Mr V. L. Bennett	8.5.58
Pargeter Bob Up	Blenheim	D	Ch. Abelard of Ttuweh	Ch. Pargeter Phyllida	Breeder	Mrs D. Keswick	7.1.58
1961							
Vairire Charmaine of Crisdig	Blenheim	B	Ch. Sunninghill Perseus of Loch Fee	Vairire Candida	Mrs J. R. Burgess	Mrs E. R. Burroughes	4.1.59
Bowstones Henrietta	Tricolour	B	Goldicote Bonzo of Crustadele	Bowstones Trudi	Breeder	Mrs I. Booth	21.6.59
Oyster Pattie of Ttuweh	Blenheim	B	Mars of Ttuweh	Pearl Blaze of Loch Fee	Mrs A. Pitt	Lady Anderson	10.10.57
Samuel of Sunninghill	Tricolour	D	Amulet of Sunninghill	Barings Sara of Chandlers	Major Aubrey-Fletcher	Miss P. Turle	9.6.57

Name	Colour	Sex	Sire	Dam	Owner	Breeder	Date of Birth
Rekalb Moss Rose	Blenheim	B	Ch. Orlando of Goldicote	Pargeter Rose	Breeder	Mrs N. V. Blacker	11.7.59
Cornlands Mistress Anne of Manscross	Blenheim	B	Maniken of Manscross	Manscross Peggy of Pern	Mrs D.P. Rae	Dr and Mrs K. C. Mackenzie	11.5.58
1962 Barings Fortescue	Tricolour	D	Ch. Aloysius of Sunninghill	Barings Angela	Breeder	Mrs M. Patten	3.8.59
Malcolm of Lenharra	Blenheim	D	Ch. Aloysius of Sunninghill	Belinda of Lenharra	Breeder	Mrs L. White	22.4.59
Trambitops Madame Louise	Tricolour	B	Ch. Aloysius of Sunninghill	Perle of Lenharra	Mrs B. Sheridan	Mrs M. H. Bartels	7.8.57
Sebastian of Eyeworth	Blenheim	D	Ch. Clarion of Eyeworth	Nymphia of Eyeworth	Breeder	Lady Forwood	25.1.59
Roulette of Temple Hill	Blenheim	B	Ch. Raoul of Ttiweh	Rhea of Eyeworth	Mrs G. B. Biddle	Mrs P. Eccles	10.4.59
Cerdric of Ttiweh	Blenheim	D	Pound Foolish of Ttiweh	Britannia of Ttiweh	Breeder	Mrs A. Pitt	30.9.59
Waterston Chanticleer	Blenheim	D	Ch. Clarion of Eyeworth	Ch. Trambitops Madame Louise	Breeder	Mrs B. Sheridan	22.9.60

Name	Colour	Sex	Sire	Dam	Breeder	Owner	Date
Amanda of Little Breach	Blenheim	B	Ch. Hillbarn Quixote	Wendy of Hillbarn	Breeder	Mrs L. R. Percival	8.1.58
Amelia of Laguna	Blenheim	B	Ch. Aloysius of Sunninghill	Pargeter Paprika	Mrs F. Cryer	Miss L. McKay	22.1.59
Mingshang Danby	Tricolour	D	Hillbarn Daniel	Mingshang Alexandra	Mrs I. J. Green	Miss P.M. Mayhew	16.5.60

1963

Name	Colour	Sex	Sire	Dam	Breeder	Owner	Date
Mimi of Eyeworth	Blenheim	B	Ch. Sebastian of Eyeworth	Eyeworth Midinette of Knightlow	Breeder	Lady Forwood	6.9.60
Barings Claramara	Black/Tan	B	Tiuweh Torquil O'Cockpen	Barings Sara of Chandlers	Mrs M. Patten	Mrs V. Preece	10.2.58
Edward of Knightlow	Blenheim	D	Kingmaker of Tiuweh	Musette of Knightlow	Mrs S. Halsall	Mrs E. Barnett	22.9.61
Cointreau of Eyeworth	Black/Tan	D	Jupiter of Eyeworth	Baccante of Eyeworth	Breeder	Lady Forwood	10.9.56
Cordelian Pargeter Up Jenkins	Blenheim	B	Ch. Pargeter Bob Up	Pearl Blaze of Loch Fee	Mr J. P. Middleton	Mrs A. Pitt	2.8.60
Welland Valley Alcibiades of Goldicote	Blenheim	D	Ch. Yadipati of Goldicote	Welland Valley Aphrodite	Mrs R. Pilkington	Mr and Mrs P. H. Tregoning	9.6.60
Bettina of Little Breach	Blenheim	B	Ch. Hillbarn Quixote	Wendy of Hillbarn	Breeder	Mrs L. R. Percival	10.2.59
Dickon of Little Breach	Blenheim	D	Hillbarn Fabion	Ch. Amanda of Little Breach	Breeder	Mrs L. R. Percival	1.2.60
Pargeter Melissa	Blenheim	B	Ch. Cerdic of Tiuweh	Pargeter Polyantha of Goldicote	Breeder	Mrs D. Keswick	13.5.61

Name	Colour	Sex	Sire	Dam	Owner	Breeder	Date of Birth
1964 Barings Margareta	Black/Tan	B	Ch. Barings Fortescue	Ch. Barings Claramara	Mrs E. Booth	Mrs M. Patten	7.3.62
Crisdig Celebration	Blenheim	D	Crisdig Henry	Vairire Venetia of Crisdig	Breeder	Mrs J. R. Burgess	20.2.62
Cantella of Eyeworth	Tricolour	B	Chello of Eyeworth	Baccante of Eyeworth	Mr and Mrs C. Cooke	Lady Forwood	16.11.61
Otterholt Cold Cream	Blenheim	B	Charles O'Cockpen	Otterholt Cowslip of Eyeworth	Breeder	Miss B. M. Miller	30.12.61
Crisdig Charm	Blenheim	B	Crisdig Henry	Vairire Venetia of Crisdig	Breeder	Mrs J. R. Burgess	20.2.62
Charlotte of Little Breach	Blenheim	B	Ch. Hillbarn Quixote	Wendy of Hillbarn	Mr and Mrs C. Cooke	Mrs L. R. Percival	13.8.60
Don Miguel of Kormar	Black/Tan	D	Ramon of Kormar	Kathalan	Miss M. Marshall	Mrs K. G. Plowright	15.10.58
Pargeter Trillium of Ttweh	Blenheim	D	Ch. Cerdric of Ttiweh	Pargeter Polynia	Mrs A. Pitt	Mrs D. Keswick	15.4.63
1965 Welland Valley Ignatius of Kormar	Tricolour	D	Ch. Aloysius of Sunninghill	Rekalb Nada	Mr R. G. Matthews	Mrs D. Isitt	14.5.59

Name	Colour	Sex	Sire	Dam	Breeder	Owner	Date
Alexis of Janton	Tricolour	D	Ch. Welland Valley Ignatius of Kormar	Janton Philomena	Breeder	Mrs Fox Carter	30.7.60
Pilar of Pield	Blenheim	B	Ch. Mingshang Dandy	Ch. Charlotte of Little Breach	Breeder	Mr and Mrs C. M. Cooke	13.9.62
Vairire Duchess Xenia of Santander	Blenheim	B	Ch. Cerdric of Ttiweh	Vairire Isis	Mr and Mrs I. W. Taylor	Mrs E. R. Burroughes	14.12.62
Clohamon Heatherbell of Loch Fee	Blenheim	B	Ch. Sunninghill Perseus of Loch Fee	Clohamon Brownie	Mrs E. J. Nugent	Lady Levinge	26.1.61
Caplode Candy of Maxholt	Blenheim	D	Captain of Dendy	Sarah of Mayholt	Mrs K. M. Rickett	Mrs M. Talbot	6.5.62
Discus of Eyeworth	Blenheim	D	Pargeter Fling	Polka of Eyeworth	Breeder	Lady Forwood	11.7.64

1966

Name	Colour	Sex	Sire	Dam	Breeder	Owner	Date
Sugar Crisp of Ttiweh	Blenheim	D	Ch. Edward of Knightlow	Pearl Blaze of Loch Fee	Breeder	Mrs A. Pitt	16.5.63
Hillbarn Harriet	Blenheim	B	Ch. Dickon of Little Breach	Camilla of Hillbarn	Mrs L. R. Percival	Mr L. R. Percival	4.12.62
Crisdig Candid	Blenheim	B	Crisdig Henry	Vairire Venetia of Crisdig	Breeder	Mrs J. R. Burgess	20.2.62
Vairire Osiris	Blenheim	D	Ch. Cerdric of Ttiweh	Vairire Isis	Miss J. Douglas	Mrs E. R. Burroughes	14.12.62
Timja Clarinet	Blenheim	D	Duke of Crustadele	Ch. Crisdig Candid	Mrs D. Murray	Mrs E. J. Young	20.9.63

Name	Colour	Sex	Sire	Dam	Owner	Breeder	Date of Birth
Heatherside Perry	Blenheim	D	Heatherside Hamish	Heatherside Tutti	Breeder	Mrs I. J. Green	20.10.62
Pargeter Myrrhis	Blenheim	B	Ch. Pargeter Bob Up	Ch. Pargeter Melissa	Breeder	Mrs D. Keswick	1.8.64
Pargeter McBounce	Blenheim	D	Ch. Pargeter Bob Up	Ch. Pargeter Melissa	Breeder	Mrs D. Keswick	1.8.64
Millstone Alleluia of Sunninghill	Tricolour	B	Ch. Aloysius of Sunninghill	Sunninghill Leisure Hour of Ttiweh	Miss P. Turle	Mrs E. Booth	31.10.61
Crisdig Merry Matelot	Blenheim	D	Ch. Crisdig Celebration	Ch. Vairire Charmaine of Crisdig	Breeder	Mrs J. R. Burgess	1.12.64
Imp of Crombie	Blenheim	D	Pargeter Fling	Alma of Crombie	Breeder	Mr G. Crawford	24.12.62
1967 Heatherside Ailie	Tricolour	B	Ch. Mingshang Danby	Heatherside Verily	Breeder	Mrs I. J. Green	14.9.63
Bowstones Brigid	Tricolour	B	Bowstones Bobdink	Bowstones Mirabelle	Mrs J. Booth	Mrs S. Law	11.8.64
Cherry Court Wake Robin	Blenheim	D	Pargeter Trillium of Ttiweh	Ch. Pargeter Melissa	Breeder	Mrs R. Stenning	1.8.64
Eyeza Crisdig Pip	Blenheim	D	Crisdig Jasper	Vairire Venetia of Crisdig	Miss L. Parker	Mrs J. R. Burgess	6.12.64

1968

Bowstones Victoria of Little Breach	Tricolour	B	Ch. Barings Fortescue	Bowstones Piprage	Mrs L. R. Percival	Mrs J. Booth	30.4.62
Carmen O'Cockpen	Blenheim	B	Ch. Mingshang Danby	Carol O'Cockpen	Breeder	Lt. Col. H. G. C. Laird	25.6.64
Crisdig Geordie of Ottermouth	Blenheim	D	Ch. Pargeter Bob Up	Ch. Vairire Charmaine of Crisdig	Mrs Biddle	Mrs J. R. Burgess	7.4.63
Crisdig Harlequin	Tricolour	D	Ch. Crisdig Celebration	Crisdig Salome	Breeder	Mrs J. R. Burgess	4.12.64
Odette of Little Breach	Blenheim	B	Littlebreach Pepe of Pield	Ch. Harriet of Hillbarn	Breeder	Mrs L. R. Percival	19.10.66
Pargeter Dusty Answer	Blenheim	D	Pargeter Moonduster	Pargeter Catriona	Breeder	Mrs B. Keswick	5.10.66
Prunella of Maxholt	Tricolour	B	Bowstones Peter	Ophelia of Gorsedene	Breeder	Mrs M. M. Talbot	4.11.62
Startime of Staffold	Black/Tan	B	Ch. Welland Valley Ignatius of Kormar	Starlet of Staffold	Mrs G. E. Garratley	R. G. Matthews	21.3.64
Tnegun Flavia	Blenheim	B	Minstrel of Sunninghill	Tnegun Florabell	Breeder	Mrs C. J. Nugent	11.11.63

1969

Alansmere McGoogans Maggie May	Blenheim	B	Ch. McGoogans Ruari	Magenta of Crustadele	Messrs Hall and Evans	Mrs C. Kirkpatrick	8.12.66

Name	Colour	Sex	Sire	Dam	Owner	Breeder	Date of Birth
Angel's Song of Ttiweh	Blenheim	B	Ch. Cerdric of Ttiweh	Angelique of Ttiweh	Breeder	Mrs A. Pitt	15.3.66
Archie McMuck of Eyeworth	Blenheim	D	Int. Ch. Pargeter McBounce	Polka of Eyeworth	Breeder	Lady Forwood	20.7.67
Crisdig Rapture	Blenheim	B	Ch. Crisdig Celebration	Crisdig Genevieve	Mrs D. J. Williams	Mrs J. R. Burgess	3.1.65
Heatherside Fortune	Tricolour	D	Doghill Doughnut	Heatherside Veronica	Breeder	Mrs I. J. Green	23.4.65
Josephine of Blagreaves	Tricolour	B	Ch. Barings Fortescue	Blagreaves Boadicea of Ttiweh	Breeder	Miss B. M. Palfree	21. 3. 64
McGoogans Ruari	Blenheim	D	Crisdig Jasper	Bella of Flowershill	Breeder	Mrs C. Kirkpatrick	25.1.65
Piccola of Crustadele	Ruby	B	Ch. Timja Clarinet	Minnack Piccolo	Breeder	Mrs D. J. Murray	23.2.65
Ring a Ding of Ottermouth	Blenheim	D	Barcarole of Crustadele	Reinette of Crustadele	Miss J. Files	Mrs Biddle	19.11.66
SerenLight of Staffold	Tricolour	D	Ch. Welland Valley Ignatius of Kormar	Soft Lights of Staffold	Breeder	Mr R. G. Matthews	5.9.66
Tnegun Rebound	Blenheim	D	Int. Ch. Pargeter McBounce	Tnegun Flavia	Breeder	Mrs E. Nugent	15.5.66

	Colour	Sex	Sire	Dam	Breeder	Owner	Date
1970							
Corwick Amber of Little Breach	Blenheim	B	Ch. Heatherside Fortune	Olga of Littlebreach	Mrs L. R. Percival	Mrs Wicker	13.4.68
Edgebourne Red Rake of Caplode	Ruby	D	Caplode Lavren (Alexandrite)	His Mischief of Edgebourne	Mrs Rickett and Mr E. A. Edgeton-Williams	Lt-Cmdr and Mrs Edgeton-Williams	
Ivan The Terrible of Chacombe	Black/Tan	D	Ruy Evanlyn of Kormar	Belle of Kormar	Breeder	Mrs S. Schilizzi	21.4.67
Millstone Crisdig Joy	Tricolour	B	Ch. Crisdig Harlequin	Crisdig Lammeseve of Sunninghill	Mrs J. R. Burgess	Mrs E. M. Booth	29.9.66
Rose Mary of Ottermouth	Blenheim	B	Ch. Vairire Osiris	Rosette of Ottermouth	Breeder	Mrs Biddle	20.7.67
Rose Mullion of Ottermouth	Blenheim	D	Ch. Vairire Osiris	Rosette of Ottermouth	Breeder	Mrs Biddle	20.7.67
Rupurts Bonita	Blenheim	B	Ch. Caplode Candy of Maxholt	Rose-Marie of Eyeworth	Breeder	Mr Shaw	11.7.67
Stellers Eider of Pantisa	Ruby	D	Ttiweb Black Prince of Cockpen	Cuckoo of Pantisa	Mrs Kirkpatrick	Mrs Halsall	31.8.68
Gleamer of Pantisa	Blenheim	B	Corn on the Cob of Pantisa	Simone of Pantisa	Breeder	Mrs Halsall	16.11.68
1971							
Cherrycourt Patrick of Maxholt	Blenheim	D	Ch. Cherrycourt Wake Robin	Bridget of Cherrycourt	Mrs.Talbot	Mrs R. Stenning	30.12.65

Name	Colour	Sex	Sire	Dam	Owner	Breeder	Date of Birth
Crisdig Ragamuffin	Tricolour	B	Crisdig Mr Patch	Ch. Crisdig Charm	Breeder	Mrs J. R. Burgess	6.6.69
McGoogans Floraida	Blenheim	B	Ch. McGoogans Ruari	McGoogans Luck of the Irish	Breeder	Mrs C. Kirkpatrick	1.6.67
Requiem of Ottermouth	Blenheim	D	Barcarole of Crustadele	Reinette of Ottermouth	Breeder	Mrs G. Biddle	19.11.66
Crisdig Buttons	Blenheim	B	Ch. Crisdig Merry Matelot	Crisdig Trinket	Breeder	Mrs J. R. Burgess	9.12.67
Roblenbel Crisdig Constellation	Blenheim	B	Ch. Crisdig Merry Matelot	Crisdig Genevieve	Mrs H. McAllister	Mrs J. R. Burgess	16.9.68
Prince Rudolph of Scwalfa	Blenheim	D	Gayela Randolph Prima	Egama Berlinetta	Mrs Obo	Mr M. B. Morgan	7.5.69
Lance of Beamshaw	Tricolour	D	Master Richard of Nizmat	Ianthe of Hillbarn	Breeder	Mr and Mrs Wood	27.9.68
Bowstones Dita	Tricolour	B	Wishwin Agustas	Bowstones Pargeter Bellement	Breeder	Mrs J. Booth	5.3.67
1972 Gaydew Gaiety	Blenheim	B	Eyeza Crisdig Pip	Gaydew Giee	Breeder	Miss D. E. Wilson	13.12.68
Homer Brent Lindy Lou	Blenheim	B	Ch. Rose Mullion of Otterholt	Homerbrent Harmony	Breeder	Mrs Coaker	5.3.71

Name	Sex	Colour	Sire	Dam	Breeder	Owner	Date
Huntsback Solitaire	D	Blenheim	Ch. Heatherside Fortune	Crisdig Rapture	Breeder	D. E. Williams	25.10.68
Ottermouth Back Badge	D	Tricolour	Ch. Crisdig Harlequin	Ch. Rose Mary of Ottermouth	Breeder	Mrs G. G. Biddle	4.7.70
Sartorius Sebastian of Eyeworth	D	Blenheim	Can. Ch. Pickle of Crustadele	Gorgeous Gussie of Eyeworth	Lady Forwood and Baron Tournaye d'Asten	Baron Tournaye d'Asten	16.12.68
Snow Crystal of Aldersbrook	B	Blenheim	Lochbuie Crisdig Touchstone	Crisdig Charity of Aldersbrook	Breeder	Mrs R. U. Hart	23.2.69
Tnegun Charivari	D	Blenheim	Ch. Crisdig Celebration	Tnegun Florabell	Breeder	Mrs E. J. Nugent	6.7.68
Venetia of Littlebreach	B	Tricolour	Bowstones Dougal of Littlebreach	Odette of Littlebreach	Mrs S. Schilizzi	Mrs L. R. Percival	4.4.70
1973 Alansmere Aquarius	D	Blenheim	Ch. Vairire Osiris	Ch. Alansmere McGoogans Maggie May	Breeder	Messrs Hall and Evans	10.9.71
Homerbrent Minstrel	D	Triedous	Ch. Requiem of Ottermouth	Homerbrent Nolana	Breeder	Mrs Coaker	31.10.70
Jia Amphion	D	Blenheim	Horatio of Beamshaw	Bowstones Dominique of Jia	Mrs D. C. Archer	Miss J. Archer	2.6.71
Kershope Sandon Park Icebreaker	D	Blenheim	Int. Ch. Pargeter McBounce	Sandon Park Crystal	Miss C. Gatheral	Mrs Park	19.1.72

Name	Colour	Sex	Sire	Dam	Owner	Breeder	Date of Birth
Sunninghill Broomsquire of Waterston	Blenheim	D	Banneret of Sunninghill	Rose Carillon of Sunningdale	Miss P. Turle and Mrs Hewett	Miss P. Turle	2.12.70
McGoogans Eideard	Ruby	D	Ch. Stellers Eider of Pantisa	Ch. Piccola of Crustadele	Breeder	Mr and Mrs D. G. Gillies	31.7.70
Brendonvale Serena of Tuweh	Blenheim	B	Ttiweh Granaldon Maigret	Toffee of Buckney	Mr and Mrs A. Bradley-Reynolds	Mrs A. Pitt	22.12.68
His Sunset of Edgebourne	Ruby	B	Caplode Lavren Alexandrite	His Mischief of Edgebourne	Mrs E. Slightam	Lt-Cdr and Mrs Edgeton-Williams	22.8.67
Crisdig Florida	Blenheim	B	Int. Ch. Pargeter McBounce	Ch. Crisdig Buttons	Breeder	Mrs J. R. Burgess	18.7.70
Ashpenda Only Me of Maxholt	Tricolour	B	Minstrel Boy of Maxholt	Ashpenda Sweet Martini	Mrs M. M. Talbot	Mrs C. Duffield	22.5.71
Tnegun Diamante	Blenheim	B	Ir. Ch. Tnegun Priam	Desire of Ttiweh	Breeder	Mrs E. J. Nugent	10.5.69
1974							
Brendonvale Mirabelle	Blenheim	B	Ch. Rose Mullion of Ottermouth	Bredonvale Ttiweh Lavengro	Messrs Hall and Evans	Mr and Mrs A. Bradley-Reynolds	5.1.71.
Crisdig Cornish Caper	Blenheim	B	Ch. Crisdig Merry Matelot	Lansola Love Story of Eyeworth	Mrs J. R. Burgess	Miss C. M. Dustow	4.8.71

Name	Colour	Sex	Sire	Dam	Breeder	Owner	Date
Crisdig Prospect	Blenheim	B	Int Ch. Pargeter McBounce	Ch. Crisdig Buttons	Miss V. H. Salmon	Mrs J. R. Burgess	18.7.70
Homerbrent Captivation	Tricolour	B	Homerbrent Crisdig Reflection	Homerbrent Nolana	Miss A. Coaker	Mrs K. M. Coaker	10.9.71
Homerbrent Samantha	Blenheim	B	Homerbrent Highlander	Homerbrent Annadrewan	Mrs K. M. Coaker	Mrs P. Mawe	25.8.72
Leynsord Salutation	Blenheim	D	Rosemar Ulysses of Leynsord	Leynsord Barleycorn	Breeder	Mr and Mrs D. W. Reynolds	25.10.72
Maxholt Veryon	Tricolour	D	Ch. Cherrycourt Patrick of Maxholt	Victoriana of Maxholt	Breeder	Mrs J. Talbot	21.5.71
Millstone Beechking Tansy	Black/Tan	B	Millstone Eustace	Highstead Renee	Mrs E. M. Booth	Mr and Mrs R. Clark	17.6.70
Mintrode Sheenagh of Maxholt	Tricolour	B	Minstrel Boy of Maxholt	Dalginross Rosalind	Mesdames Talbot and Barwell	Mrs E. Ord	6.10.71
Mr Softie of Pantisa	Tricolour	D	Jester of Pantisa	Pearlie of Pantisa	Mr G. Donaldson	Mrs S. Halsall	12.3.71
Romulus of Beamshaw	Tricolour	D	Horatio of Beamshaw	Katherine of Little Breach	Breeder	Mr R. W. Wood	18.4.71
Tnegun Marieanne	Blenheim	B	Coram of Sunninghill	Tnegun Merrybell	Breeder	Mrs E. J. Nugent	15.8.71

1975

Name	Colour	Sex	Sire	Dam	Breeder	Owner	Date
Brunor Yorkshire Lad	Blenheim	D	Int Ch. Pargeter McBounce	Brunor Anabel	Breeder	Mr and Mrs L. Irons	18.12.72

Name	Colour	Sex	Sire	Dam	Owner	Breeder	Date of Birth
Chandlers Phalaris	Black/Tan	D	Chandlers Mornington	Chandlers Phaedra	Breeder	Mrs G. Preece	29.9.67
Cordelia of Chacombe	Ruby	B	Ruy Evanlyn of Kormar	Belle of Kormar	Breeder	Mrs S. Schilizzi	21.4.67
Heatherside Candida	Tricolour	B	Heatherside Bowstones Gareth	Heatherside Charlotte	Mrs P. Martin	Mrs I. J. Green	10.9.70
Lansola Cornish Settler of Crisdig	Tricolour	D	Ch. Crisdig Harlequin	Crustadele Iseult of Lansola	Mrs J. R. Burgess	Miss C. M. Dustow	18.3.73
Mintrode Fred of Maxholt	Tricolour	D	Minstrel Boy of Maxholt	Dalginross Rosalind	Mrs J. Talbot	Mrs E. Ord	22.5.72
Rupurts Ivanhoe	Blenheim	D	Minstrel Boy of Maxholt	Ch. Rupurts Bonita	Mrs P. M. Stark	Mr A. J. Shaw	14.12.70
Starwell Dusky of McGoogans	Ruby	B	Ch. Stellers Eider of Pantisa	Starwell Dinah	Mr and Mrs R. Lilley	Mrs Ricketts	29.12.70
Tregarron Tanya's Kathy	Blenheim	B	Homerbrent Crisdig Reflection	Harrowbeer Charmaine	Breeder	Miss B. M. Dowd	22.4.72
Astraddle Fame 'n' Fortune	Blenheim	B	Heatherside Bowstones Gareth	Ballydare Bella	Breeder	Mrs B. Stanley	22.3.71
Kershope Rebound	Blenheim	D	Int. Ch. Pargeter McBounce	Pargeter Mahonia	Breeder	Miss C. L. M. Gatheral	1.9.71

Name	Colour	Sex	Sire	Dam	Breeder	Owner	Date
Roblenbel My Love	Blenheim	B	Int Ch. Pargeter McBounce	Ch. Roblenbel Crisdig Constellation	Breeder	Mrs McAllister	2.10.71
1976							
Crisdig Leading Seaman	Blenheim	D	Ch. Crisdig Merry Matelot	Ch. Crisdig Florida	Breeder	Mrs J. R. Burgess	14.10.73
Homaranne Andy Capp	Tricolour	D	Bonnyglen Jasper of Blagreaves	Ch. Homerbrent Captivation	Mrs K. M. Coaker	Miss M. A. Coaker	16.11.73
Jia Egeria	Blenheim	B	Breklaw Challenger	Jia Lady Camilla	Breeder	Mrs D. Archer	13.6.74
Mintrode Jotham of Maxholt	Tricolour	D	Minstrel Boy of Maxholt	Dalginross Rosalind	Mrs J. Talbot	Mrs E. Ord	24.5.74
Prosperpina of Sunninghill	Blenheim	B	Ch. Sunninghill Broomsquire of Waterston	Sunninghill Pepita	Breeder	Miss P. Turle	19.12.74
Sarvessa Lord Jim	Tricolour	D	Ch. Kershope Sandon Park Icebreaker	Wedding Bells of Maxholt	Breeder	Mr G. Walker	2.1.74
Ttiweh Rosanna	Blenheim	B	Ch. Rose Mullion of Ottermouth	Ttiweh Last Rose	Mrs G. Biddle	Mrs A. Pitt	19.7.73
1977							
Crisdig Virtue of Bredonvale	Blenheim	B	Ch. Crisdig Merry Matelot	Ch. Crisdig Ragamuffin	Messrs Hall and Evans	Mrs J. R. Burgess	14.2.72
Cadeyrn Black Tulip	Black/Tan	D	Rhosnessney Prince Ivan of Rhybank	Laughernbrook April Love	Breeder	Mrs J. E. Watts	1.7.74

Name	Colour	Sex	Sire	Dam	Owner	Breeder	Date of Birth
Hazelbury Coppelia	Blenheim	B	Lochbuie Dandini	Applecourt Flippant of Hazelbury	Breeder	Mr and Mrs R. T. G. Ford	2.9.72
Chandlers Roberta	Ruby	B	Lansola Petroc of Elah	Chandlers Royal Rhoda	Breeder	Mrs G. Preece	19.7.72
Brunor Mary Rose	Blenheim	B	Ch. Rose Mullion of Ottermouth	Brunor Christmas Carol	Breeder	Mr and Mrs L. Irons	7.1.73
Heidi of Homerbrent	Tricolour	B	Homerbrent Highlander	Glynvale Hannah	Mrs K. M. Coaker	Mrs Handley	25.8.75
Bowstones Zelma	Tricolour	B	Bowstones Ambrose	Bowstones Ruella	Mrs J. Booth	Mr and Mrs V. Wadwell	10.8.74
Chacombe Alexis	Tricolour	D	Jaimie of Littlebreach	Ch. Venetia of Littlebreach	Breeder	Mrs S. Schilizzi	30.7.73
Homerbrent Samson	Blenheim	D	Int. Ch. Thegun Charivari	Ch. Homerbrent Samantha	Breeder	Mrs K. M. Coaker	16.10.75
1978 Chacombe Camilla	Ruby	B	Ch. Edgebourne Red Rake of Caplode	Ch. Cordelia of Chacombe	Breeder	Mrs S. Schilizzi	12.7.74
Kindrum Carousel	Blenheim	B	Kindrum Roulette	Kindrum Candida	Breeder	Mrs D. Thornhill	5.7.75

Name	Colour	Sex	Sire	Dam	Breeder	Owner	Date
Charlottetown None So Fair	Tricolour	B	Charlottetown Inigo Jones	Fenella of Charlottetown	Breeder	Mrs S. V. Barwell	19.10.73
McGoogans Chantal	Blenheim	B	Farne Silver Shadow of McGoogans	McGoogans Ruan	Mr C. A. Foster	Mr and Mrs Gillies	7.10.75
Homaranne Caption	Blenheim	D	Homerbrent Henry	Ch. Homerbrent Captivation	Mrs K. M. Coaker	Miss M. A. Coaker	13.6.76
Rosemerryn of Alansmere	Blenheim	D	Ch. Rosemullion of Ottermouth	Alansmere Melody	Messrs Hall and Evans	Mrs Ings	6.9.74
Kindrum Curiosity of Criscan	Blenheim	B	Bacchus of Sunninghill	Kindrum Carlina	Mrs J. Norris	Mrs D. Thornhill	7.6.76
Amantra Bohemian Rhapsody	Tricolour	D	Ch. Homaranne Andy Capp	Alansmere Fionna Harvey	Breeder	Mrs D. Fry	3.6.76
Sheltifield Quicksilver	Blenheim	D	Sheltifield Fergus	Sheltifield Dorabella	Breeder	Mrs J. Phillips	19.10.73
Niccoli of Rhybank	Black/Tan	D	Rhosnessney Prince Ivan of Rhybank	Laughernbrook April Love	Mrs H. Fereday	Mrs J. Watts	6.8.75
Tregarron Caprice	Tricolour	B	Ch. Homaranne Andy Capp	Ch. Tregarron Tanya's Kathy	Breeder	Miss B. M. Dowd	25.6.76
Nastane Madam Cholet	Tricolour	B	Bonnyglen Jasper of Blagreaves	Pantisa Polly Flinders	Breeder	Miss A. East	16.12.74
Charlottetown Tom Jones	Tricolour	D	Minstrel Boy of Maxholt	Charlottetown Pinnacle Pot	Breeder	Mrs S. V. Barwell	.5.75

Name	Colour	Sex	Sire	Dam	Owner	Breeder	Date of Birth
1979 Alansmere Sandmartin	Blenheim	D	Ch. Rose Merryn of Alansmere	Alansmere Elgee Crystal	Breeder	Messrs A. Hall	13.4.76
Weaveley Wilma of Earlswood	Tricolour	B	Earlswood Giles	Victoria of Weaveley	Mrs R. Paris	Mrs Somerscales	6.11.74
Maxholt Christmas Carol	Blenheim	D	Towny Port of Maxholt	The Polka Dot of Maxholt	Breeder	Mrs M. Talbot	29.12.73
Kentonville Holly's Tansy	Blenheim	B	Jamie of Littlebreach	Kentonville Holly	Breeder	Mrs J. Winters	24.2.74
Jia Leartes of Tonnew	Blenheim	D	Breklaw Challenger	Jia Lady Camilla	Mr and Mrs R. Newton	Mrs D. Archer	27.9.76
Kindrum Arabella	Blenheim	B	Kindrum Roulette	Valerius Lotus Blossom	Mrs D. Thornhill	Miss Frost	19.12.76
Amantra Anchors Away	Blenheim	D	Amantra Petty Officer	Alansmere Fionna Harvey	Miss T. Fry	Mrs D. Fry	8.7.77
Salador Crystal Gayle	Blenheim	B	Salador Chelsea of Loranka	Salador Cherrybird	Breeder	Miss S. Smith	4.2.78
High Head Dolly Dimple	Blenheim	B	Homerbrent Henry	Homaranne Tammy Lin	Mrs K. M. Coaker and Mrs J. Huggon	Mrs J. Huggon	18.4.76

Name	Sex	Colour	Sire	Dam	Breeder	Owner	Date
Huntsbank Vagabond	D	Blenheim	Astraddle Sign'n'Ara	Hillyacres Vanity Fair	Breeder	Mr D. G. Williams	6.4.78
1980							
Sunninghill Rigadoon of Highcurley	D	Blenheim	Ch. Rose Mullion of Ottermouth	Rose Pavane of Sunninghill	Mrs P. C. Rooney	Miss P. Turle	3.75
Alansmere Michelle	B	Blenheim	Ch. Alansmere Sandmartin	Ch. Bredonvale Mirabelle	Breeders	Messrs Hall & Evans	1.78
Peatland Flora Jenson	B	Blenheim	Ch. Homaranne Caption	Pantisa Saab	Breeder	Mrs M. Millican	4.78
Jia Mercury of Tonnew	D	Blenheim	Ch. Chacombe Alexis	Ch. Jia Egeria	Mr & Mrs R. C. Newton	Mrs D. Archer	12.77
Sweet Seraphim of Amantra	B	Tricolour	Ch. Homaranne Andy Capp	Alansmere Fionna Harvey	Mrs D. Fry	Messrs Hall & Evans	7.75
Wolvershill Hannah	B	Ruby	Ch. Cadeyrn Black Tulip	Highstead Hosannah of Wolvershill	Breeder	Mrs D. E. Martin	12.76
Alansmere Rosetta of Crieda	B	Blenheim	Ch. Alansmere Sandmartin	Ch. Bredonvale Mirabelle	Mr B. Field	Messrs Hall & Evans	9.78
Crisdig Ted	B	Blenheim	Ch. Crisdig Leading Seaman	Ranee of Jann-Graye of Crustadele	Breeder	Mrs J. R. Burgess	12.78
Crisdig Peace of Volney	B	Blenheim	Ch. Crisdig Leading Seaman	Crisdig Call Me Madam	Miss M. J. & Mrs T. V. Boardman	Mrs J. R. Burgess	9.75

Name	Colour	Sex	Sire	Dam	Owner	Breeder	Date of Birth
Dill of High Head	Blenheim	B	Aust. Ch. Homerbrent Henry	Homaranne Tammy Lin	Breeder	Mrs J. Huggon	4.76
Karabel Caprice	Black/Tan	B	Ch. Niccoli of Rhybank	Karabel Tamarisk	Breeder	Mrs J. M. Blunt	8.77
Hazelbury Crispin	Tricolour	D	Hazelbury Gulliver	Hazelbury Quickstep	Breeders	Mr & Mrs R. T. G. Ford	8.76
1981 Millstone Folly of Magien	Blenheim	B	Dunhelm the Admiral	Millstone Melba	M. H. & J. A. Stroud	Miss S. Mills	2.79
Amantra Roxy Music	Tricolour	D	Eng. & Aust. Ch. Amantra Bohemian Rhapsody	Withycombe Carlotta	Mrs D. & Miss T. Fry	Mrs Clarke	12.78
Ronnoc Rhum of Sancem	Blenheim	D	Ronnoc True Luck	Ronnoc Pollinella	Mrs K. M. Coaker	Mr Connor	9.77
Crisdig Marion	Blenheim	B	Ch. Amantra Anchors Away	Crisdig Georgia	Breeder	Mrs J. R. Burgess	1.79
Amantra Bohemian Image	Tricolour	B	Eng. & Aust. Ch. Amantra Bohemian Rhapsody	Nufus Christmas Rose	Mrs D. Fry	Mrs J. Ferriday	11.78
Kentonville Fern's Son	Blenheim	D	Ch. Chacombe Alexis	Kentonville Fern	Breeder	Mrs J. Winters	10.75

Name	Colour	Sex	Sire	Dam	Breeder	Owner	Date
Ricksbury Only Charm	Blenheim	B	Ch. Homaranne Caption	Ricksbury Cool Charm	Breeders	Messrs Rix & Berry	11.79
Pinewood Snowflake	Blenheim	B	Ch. Homaranne Caption	Pinewood Snoopy	Breeders	Mr & Mrs L. F. Priestley	1.79
Maxholt Jack in the Box	Tricolour	D	Ch. Maxholt Christmas Carol	Ch. Mintrode Sheenagh of Maxholt	Breeder	Mrs M. M. Talbot	6.77
Paulian Bracken	Blenheim	D	Syretta Bracken	Lady Gay of Meldon	Mrs Sidgwick	Mrs Stokoe	10.76
Little Breach Zachary of Chacombe	Tricolour	D	Ch. Chacombe Alexis	Little Breach Xanthe	Mrs D. Schilizzi	Mrs L. R. Percival	7.78
Hurleaze Naughty But Nice	Blenheim	B	Ch. Homaranne Caption	Tayfern Guinevere of Hurleaze	Breeder	Mrs D. Hurley	9.79
1982 Salador Coppergleam	Ruby	B	Salador Charlock	Salador Cascade	Breeder	Miss S. E. Smith	17.7.79
Kindrum Sylvia	Blenheim	B	Kindrum Barnacle Bill	Kindrum Cosy	Miss E. Thornhill	Mrs D. Thornhill	31.3.78
Astraddle Edinglen Caravino	Blenheim	D	Astraddle Sigh'n'Ara	Edinglen Silver Jubilee	Mrs B. Stanley	Mrs Arnold	23.1.79
Fontelania Capricious	Tricolour	B	Farne Silver Shadow of McGoogans	Fontelania Cameiro	Breeder	Mr & Mrs A. J. Milton	9.2.79
Salador Celtic Prince	Tricolour	D	Salador Chelsea of Loranka	Salador Cherrybird	Breeder	Miss S. E. Smith	12.5.81

Name	Colour	Sex	Sire	Dam	Owner	Breeder	Date of Birth
Parkwall Horizon	Blenheim	D	Ch. Crisdig Ted	Parkwall Maid of Mourne	Breeder	Mrs J. Owens	10.3.80
Salador Crystabelle	Blenheim	B	Ch. Homerbrent Samson	Ch. Salador Crystal Gayle	Breeder	Miss S. E. Smith	22.8.80
Homerbrent Pegasus	Blenheim	D	Arkle of Homerbrent	Lobb Bathsheba	Mrs K. M. Coaker	Mrs Bater	16.4.78
Homerbrent Bewitched	Blenheim	B	Ch. Homaranne Caption	Ch. Homerbrent Samantha	Breeder	Mrs K. M. Coaker	27.3.79
Baridene Royal Serenade of Charlesworth	Tricolour	D	Kindrum Barnacle Bill	Baridene Sweet Serenade	Miss C. G. Greenall	Mrs J. Gough	23.9.78
Cottismeer Gem Signet	Blenheim	B	Ch. Homerbrent Samson	Leynsord Velvet Glove of Cottismeer	Breeder	Mrs L. Higgins	26.6.79
Tabitha of Tayfern	Blenheim	B	Ch. Rupurts Ivanhoe	Bernadene of Cardsfarm	Mrs P. Stark	Mrs Adamson	13.5.78
Kindrum Rose Red	Ruby	B	Kindrum Jiminy Cricket	Kindrum Victoria Plum	Mr G. Porter	Mrs D. Thornhill	30.10.78
Crieda Rosella	Blenheim	B	Ch. Homaranne Caption	Ch. Alansmere Rosetta of Crieda	Breeder	Mr B. Field	10.80

Name	Colour	Sex	Sire	Dam	Breeder	Owner	Date
Peatland Norseman	Tricolour	D	Ch. Alansmere Sandmartin	Peatland Rebecca	Breeder	Mrs M. Millican	3.80
Cinola Super Tramp of Deeriem	Blenheim	D	Cinola Status Quo	Cinola Sheryl of Tinydels	Mrs S. Allerton	Mrs B. Evans	7.81
Jia Remus	Blenheim	D	Ch. Crisdig Ted	Ch. Jia Egeria	Breeder	Mrs D. Archer	8.80
Lanola Sister Sledge	Blenheim	B	Homerbrent Flash Harry	Amantra Narcissus	Mrs G. Ashcroft	Mr S. R. Goodwin	9.79
Naval Rating of Amantra	Blenheim	D	Amantra Naval Encounter	Amantra Wild Honey Pie	Mrs D. & Miss T. Fry	Mrs P. Shearn	7.77
Elmlin Epate	Tricolour	B	Charlottetown Mackintosh	Elmlin Electana	Breeder	Mrs A. Horan	8.81
Amantra Captain Pugwash	Blenheim	D	Aust. Ch. Amantra Starboard	Ch. Amantra Bohemian Image	Breeder	Mrs D. Fry	5.81
Highcurley Phyzz	Blenheim	D	Paper Tiger of Tanmerack	Highcurley Athena	Breeder	Mrs P. C. Rooney	8.81
Salador Crismark	Blenheim	D	Salador Clown So Happy	Salador Cascade	Breeder	Miss S. Smith	10.80
Astraddle Cause 'n'Havoc of Bowstones	Tricolour	B	Ch. Astraddle Edinglen Caravino	Astraddle Pins'n'Needles	Mrs I. Booth	Mrs B. Stanley	12.81
1984 Maibee a Misprint	Blenheim	B	Sweetbriar Billie Joe	Astra of Maplehurst	Breeder	Mrs H. Waters	12.9.81

Name	Colour	Sex	Sire	Dam	Owner	Breeder	Date of Birth
Homaranne Carson	Blenheim	D	Ch. Homaranne Caption	Homaranne Carmin	Mrs K. M. Coaker	Miss A. Coaker	6.12.80
Keelham Sweet Sarah of Cuckstool	Tricolour	B	Kilbarchans Rakes Romance	Keelham Victoria	Mrs J. Brown	Medley	27.7.79
Robinson of Crisdig	Blenheim	D	Ch. Crisdig Ted	Trixie Wyke Oliver	Mrs J. R. Burgess	M. Smale	19.5.81
Salador Celtic Maid	Blenheim	B	Ch. Salador Celtic Prince	Ch. Salador Coppergleam	Breeder	Miss S. Smith	19.9.82
Homerbrent Romeo	Blenheim	D	Eng. Ir. Ch. Ronnoc Rhum of Sancem	Ch. Homerbrent Samantha	Breeder	Mrs K. M. Coaker	9.12.81
Moorglade Mystique of Diwen	Blenheim	B	Waterston Whiplash of Tayfern	Lavren Iolanthe of Moorglade	Mrs B. Slightham	Mrs Pickett	8.2.80
Charlottetown Mackintosh	Tricolour	D	Charlottetown Wellington	Charlottetown Xtravaganza	Breeder	Mrs V. Barwell	11.11.77
Wishwin Horatio	Blenheim	D	Ch. Crisdig Ted	Wishwin Esme	Breeder	Mrs J. B. Kent	3.7.81
Homerbrent Cover Girl	Blenheim	B	Ch. Homaranne Caption	Homerbrent Shirley	Breeder	Mrs K. M. Coaker	4.9.80
Rhybank Myrhlyn	Tricolour	D	Ch. Little Breach Zachary of Chacombe	Rhybank Felicity	Breeder	Mrs C. Fereday	4.11.79

BIBLIOGRAPHY

Birchell, M. Joyce, *King Charles Spaniels* (W. & G. Foyle, 1960).
20th Century Dog. Edited by Herbert Compton (Grant Richards, 1904).
Hutchinson's Popular and Illustrated Dog Encyclopedia. Edited by Walter Hutchinson. Vol. II.
Leighton, Robert, *The New Book of the Dogs* (Cassells, 1907).
Saunders, A. C., *Jersey in the 17th Century* (Bigwood, 1931).
Stenning, M., *The Cavalier King Charles Spaniel* (W. & G. Foyle, 1964).
Stonehenge, *The Dogs of the British Islands* (Horace Cox, 1872).
Wentworth, Baroness (The Hon. Mrs Neville Lytton), *Toy Dogs and their Ancestors* (Duckworth, 1911).
Wimhurst, C. G. E., *The Book of Toy Dogs* (Frederick Muller, 1965).

INDEX